PUSHKIN
The Man and the Artist

PUSHKIN
THE MAN AND THE ARTIST

PROF. MARTHA WARREN BECKWITH
COL. PETER MALEVSKY-MALEVITCH
COL. GEORGE V. GOLOKHVASTOFF
PROF. NIKANDER STRELSKY
PROF. EDITH FAHNESTOCK
ALEXANDER S. PUSHKIN
FYODOR DOSTOYEVSKY
MRS. HELEN SHENITZ
OLIN DOWNES
BORIS BRASOL

The Black Heritage Library Collection

BOOKS FOR LIBRARIES PRESS
FREEPORT, NEW YORK
1971

Ada M. Kidder Memorial Library
Houghton College - Buffalo Campus
910 Union Road
Buffalo, N. Y. 14224

23214

First Published 1937
Reprinted 1971

Reprinted from a copy in the
Fisk University Library Negro Collection

The Poushkin Committee of America desires to express in this place its sense of extraordinary obligation to the generous cooperation of the literary contributors to this volume; as well as to the numerous friends who have helped to defray the unusual expenses of research and preparation for publication, in especial to Messrs. A. Avinoff, George M. Bodman, Boris Sergievsky, and Allen Wardwell.

INTERNATIONAL STANDARD BOOK NUMBER:
0-8369-8862-0

LIBRARY OF CONGRESS CATALOG CARD NUMBER:
75-168509

PRINTED IN THE UNITED STATES OF AMERICA

TABLE OF CONTENTS

		PAGE
I.	PUBLISHER'S PREFACE	7
II.	INTRODUCTION—*Prof. Nikander Strelsky*	9
III.	THE RENAISSANCE OF PUSHKIN—*V.*	16
IV.	A BIOGRAPHICAL SKETCH—*Col. Peter Malevsky-Malevitch*	30
V.	SPEECH DELIVERED JUNE 8, 1880—*Fyodor Dostoyevsky*	58
VI.	PUSHKIN AND RUSSIAN MUSIC—*Olin Downes*	80
VII.	THE STONE GUEST OF PUSHKIN—*Prof. Edith Fahnestock*	89
VIII.	CHAPTERS FROM "THE MIGHTY THREE"—*Boris Brasol*	99
IX.	PUSHKIN'S RELATION TO FOLKLORE—*Prof. Martha Warren Beckwith*	187
X.	PUSHKIN—HIS PLACE IN LETTERS—*Col. George V. Golokhvastoff*	205
XI.	ANTHOLOGY—*Alexander S. Pushkin*	218
XII.	BIBLIOGRAPHY—*Mrs. Helen A. Shenitz*	237

I
PUBLISHER'S PREFACE
(TO THE ORIGINAL EDITION)

WITH all the excitement associated with the worldwide celebration this year of the centenary of Pushkin's death—a celebration more wide spread than any accorded to an author in this writer's memory—very little in the way of coherent explanation for the average reader has been published in English in book form. There have appeared here a volume of almost nine hundred pages of translations of his works, a voluminous four dollar biography by Professor Ernest Simmons, addressed primarily to students, and a small volume of metrical translations of his folklore— "The Russian Wonderland" by Boris Brasol. In England, James Cleugh has written a biographical novel, "Prelude to Parnassus," which may later be republished here. That, so far as we have heard, is the complete list.

This volume is the first attempt to give the public a complete picture of "Pushkin, The Man and The Artist" in short compass at a popular price. It is written by scholars of authority, well informed as to Russian life and letters, in popular fashion. It includes a short, entertaining, readable biography, a complete English bibliography, a selection of good translations, elsewhere difficult of access, a number of short papers dealing with various important sides of the great poet's life and work, and the magnificent eulogy of Pushkin by his famous disciple, Dostoyevsky. The last was included, since so many of the contributors alluded to it, and since it was available in translation only in a small number of our more important libraries.

The publisher hopes that our public will welcome this first opportunity to acquire, with a minimum of effort, all the needed facts about a figure of worldwide interest, much discussed today. The volume is published under the supervision of The Poushkin Committee of America, for the benefit of The Poushkin Fund, Inc., the last being an American corporation for assistance to needy authors and students of the Russian language, literature, and history outside of Russia.

No attempt has been made by the publishers to unify diverse forms of spelling used by our contributors, in the case of such frequent variants as Pushkin or Poushkin, Tsar or Czar, etc., etc.

II

INTRODUCTION

To MANY Americans, this commemoration of the death of Alexander Pushkin is like laying a wreath on the tomb of the Unknown Soldier. They do it with the broad and kindly sympathy for which Americans are famous. But they are a little mystified. All the evidence points to the fact that he was a great man. But just exactly who was he?

No one will ever be able to answer this about the Unknown Soldier. He will remain forever a universal and anonymous symbol. Pushkin, too, has the distinction of being universal, but he is by no means an anonymous symbol. He is rather a living and personal endowment, not only of Russia, but of every nation, and so of everything which we call our modern culture.

You may imagine that you have never come into contact with the work of Pushkin; but that is hardly possible to-day for any literate person. Even if you have never read his work, you have seen sometime, somewhere, the print of his hand, you have heard the echo of his voice. Whatever you may have read of Russian literature owes something to him. Most of you have seen the movie

"Anna Karenina." We would not have "Anna Karenina" in either book or movie form, if it had not been for Pushkin. Most of you have heard something of Russian music. There is scarcely any great Russian composer who does not owe something to the inspiration of Pushkin.

One hundred years ago a miracle happened, when the figure of Alexander Pushkin rose like a new planet on the horizon of Russia. This Miracle is being repeated to-day, with a new intensity, a new meaning. After one hundred years, that planet is not on the wane, but in the ascendant.

All of you to-day know something of this man, even if you did not know his name a week or a month ago. There is hardly a newspaper, a magazine, with any claim to seriousness, which has not recently carried a few lines about him. They tell you that he was Russia's greatest poet. They tell you that he was the father of all Russian literature. They tell you that he shaped almost single-handed the instrument of the Russian language, and that no one since his time has played upon it with such surpassing beauty and virtuosity. They tell you, moreover, that to-day people all over the world, in colleges, in concert halls, in theatres, on the radio, are joining with Russia in honoring this man.

At first sight, this act of commemoration is astonishing. If Pushkin is Russia's first and noblest voice, why is he the last to become known abroad? Why is the Russia of the Soviets, which is now in

INTRODUCTION 11

revolt against everything which composed the external world of Pushkin, uniting in unprecedented eulogy of an aristocrat, an individualist, a man who never heard the name of Karl Marx?

The reason why he is not better known abroad, has been a problem of communication, the problem of cultural intercourse between nations. Two hundred and fifty years ago Peter the Great opened the famous "window," through which orientalized Russia looked out for the first time upon the Western nations, who thought Russia was a land of Cimmerian darkness, full of half savage barbarians. To-day, not a window, but a wide arch is flung open to East and West, revealing for the first time the complex world of the Slav. Whether you admire it or abhor it, the phenomenon of modern Russia is too dynamic, too universal in its import, to be ignored. The present of any nation is charted by its past. Pushkin was the indelible recorder of Russia's past, seen through the heart as well as through the mind, and so he was also the prophet of Russia's future.

Gogol wrote, "Pushkin is an extraordinary, perhaps a unique manifestation of the genius of the Russian people. He is a Russian in his final state of development, as he may possibly appear two hundred years hence."

Dostoyevsky said, "Pushkin created two types, Onegin and Tatiana, who sum up in themselves the most intimate secrets of Russian psychology;

with the utmost conceivable artistic skill, they represent its past and present, and indicate its future in traits of inimitable beauty."

But Pushkin was more than a great Russian. He was a great citizen of the world. Dostoyevsky said further that "he combines all human qualities, and therefore belongs to all nations, while at the same time his universality appears as a specific national trait."

Such praise reaffirms the old principle that art transcends doctrine. It testifies to the enduring value of all great art. Shakespeare understood this when he wrote the sonnet beginning:

> "Not marble, nor the gilded monuments
> of princes, shall outlive this powerful rime . . ."

And Pushkin understood it when he wrote:

> "Unto myself I reared a monument not builded
> By hands; a track thereto the people's feet will tread."

In the five glorious stanzas of this poem he looked far into the future, and he himself expressed in words, precisely and forever, why he is to-day beloved by Tsarist and Communist alike. They love him, not only for the music and the fragrance of his lines, the jewel-like perfection of their form, the soaring flight of his fantasy, but for his insight into the human heart, for the proud rebelliousness of his spirit, for his profound and genuine democ-

INTRODUCTION 13

racy, for his comprehensive grasp of reality, as sustaining and as self-renewing as the soil of his own land.

One question remains however. You will ask: if all this is true, why have we not heard of him before? We know something of the other great writers who followed him. We have read something of Tolstoy, Turgenev, Dostoyevsky. Why doesn't everybody know equally well the work of Pushkin?

The stumbling block has been the very thing which was the instrument of Pushkin's greatness, that instrument which he did so much to create—the Russian language. Flaubert, who did not know Russian, could never enjoy Pushkin in translation, in spite of everything Turgenev could say to convert him. "He is flat, your poet," replied the great Frenchman. Some of you may come away from him with the same reaction, if you sample only one or two of his lyrics. Pushkin has always been the fascination and the despair of his translators. More than one critic has declared the task a hopeless one. Yet certain passages of his work come through into English with a satisfying fullness, even if the loss in beauty and distinction is inevitable.

Prosper Merimée, who knew something of Slavic tongues, put his finger on the reason for this difficulty. Merimée declared that Pushkin's poem, "Anchar," could only be translated into Latin, because of its terseness and conciseness. In all his work there is never a superfluous word. Every one is essential and compact with meaning. For those non-Russians who have mastered Pushkin's language, his poetry and tales are their chief reward.

Before the appearance of Pushkin, Russian literature was in its infancy. With his work, it sprang into full and perfect flower. The history of world letters offers hardly a parallel to so brilliant and so sudden a growth to maturity. This fact takes on added meaning, when we reflect that his work is increasingly known and loved to-day, under conditions of life diametrically opposite to those which brought him popularity during his own lifetime. He still stands supreme, and his stature grows, just as does the body of Russian literature which he inaugurated.

Space does not permit any intimate presentation of the characteristics of Pushkin's writing in this place. Instead, I prefer to give Pushkin an opportunity to speak for himself. The eight lines I have chosen have been described as, "The inexpressible declaration of love of all the unhappy lovers of the world."

> "I loved you; even now I may confess
>   Some embers of my love their fire retain.
> But do not let it bring you more distress,
>   I do not want to sadden you again.
> Hopeless and tongue-tied, yet I loved you dearly
>   With pangs the jealous and the timid know;

So tenderly I loved you, so sincerely,
I pray, God grant another love you so."

Seven hours of daylight separate America from Moscow. Five thousand miles stretch between our eastern seaboard and the Russian frontier. There is a third kind of separation still more far-reaching. It is the difference in way of life, the difference in history—in other words, the pattern of a nation. This is what makes *foreignness*.

It is a miracle, but it is also a fact, that a single man can sometimes bridge this chasm of foreignness. Pushkin has performed this feat. The great poet has flung his bridge of words across the chasm of foreignness, across the chasm of time. In our own day, when men are searching everywhere for some kind of common denominator to draw together the nations of the world, Pushkin's songs, his fairy tales, his stories, confirm our hope of a day to come when all men, everywhere, may share, in peace and mutual understanding, the multiform experience of living.

NIKANDER STRELSKY,
Vassar College.

III

THE RENAISSANCE OF POUSHKIN

IN EVERY one of the great literatures of the world, there are one or at most two or three names, which stand at the very foundation of the literary life of the nation. These men are, in a very real sense, the founders of the nation's literature. They are not the first writers; they are not the first creative geniuses to appear in the long course of the history of the country, but they do adapt the language for all kinds of literary expression, and they first fully merge the literary forms and ideas of their people with the great stream of international literature. Dante in mediaeval Italy, Shakespeare in England, Luther in his translation of the Bible, and, still later, Lessing, Goethe, and Schiller in Germany, were men of this sort. In Russia, the name that corresponds to theirs is that of Alexander Sergeyevich Poushkin.

If this be so, as insisted on most emphatically by present-day Russians of all schools of thought and of all political parties, it may be interesting to consider why Poushkin has not as yet received that wide acclaim in other lands, which has been so generously bestowed upon him in his own. There is a widespread idea that Poushkin's works are of value only for Russia, and that, in his relations with the world outside, he is to be counted merely as another follower of Lord Byron, and is not to be considered as a great and independent figure.

The first reason for the comparative neglect of Poushkin abroad is the nature of his work. His real achievements have been buried under other forms and in many ways. Thus such productions as Boris Godounov are known primarily through the operas which have been based upon them, but the average opera attendants think only of the music, and not at all of the poet who inspired it. His prose works have been compared with those of Sir Walter Scott, without any attempt to analyze the differences in goal and method. The poems of his Byronic period have been noticed slightly. His lyric poems have usually failed of translation, or have been swept aside as personal and unimportant.

Nevertheless, the greatness of Poushkin still remains, and still awaits world recognition. The outside world must weigh Poushkin's works, and the facts of his career, before it can pass final judgment, or effectually discount the unanimous verdict of his own people.

Let us remember, then, first of all, that Poushkin is perhaps primarily a lyric poet, and that, even when he is not purely lyric, he has carried over into his other work those qualities which fundamentally mark the great lyricist. If it be true that Goethe was able to dazzle the world with his Faust, the fact remains that many of his slighter lyrics represent chiefly his mastery of the German language. So it is with Poushkin. From his earliest productions in his school days at the Lyceum, to the last poems penned shortly before his untimely death, he always manifests a perfect command of the Russian language, with a capacity for unifying the music of that tongue, and the sense of his words, into one splendid whole which defies analysis, and generally defies translation.

Only those who have attempted to translate his poems, will realize the extent to which these invisible arts and choices influence the beauty of the whole. It is easy to speak in general terms of the ideas that underlie the poems. It is hard to express the full force of the music that echoes from them. Goethe is an example of this. Everyone who knows German, knows that slight lyric, Heidenröslein; and yet the greatest poet may well be challenged to translate it without such adaptation that it becomes almost an original poem.

Poushkin has the same characteristic. He took the ordinary metres of poetry and adapted them to Russian usage, but, in so doing, he exploited to the full the Russian capacity for, and attitude towards rhyme, the possibilities of alliteration, of vowel harmony, of the use of caesuras, so that we are conscious to-day that we do not know, even in

THE RENAISSANCE 19

theory, a small part of the principles on which the poet modelled his verse. We know that he was a careful worker. We know that he studied minutely the potentialities of different forms of verse. We know that he worked in accordance with definite principles, but he never revealed them. He never, even for his friends, wrote out his ideas on Russian metrics, and to-day we can see the great difference between his command of verse and that of his greatest followers such as Lermontov; and yet we do not know the secret of the special ring and rhythm that he gave his poetry.

It was not only in his distinctive lyrics that he manifested this capacity. In his longer poems, in his metrical dramas, he used a modification of these same principles,—yes, even in his prose, for the prose of Poushkin is as unique in Russian literature as is his verse. Everywhere and in every thing he wrote, he employed this special command of the language, and thus he created the mass of artistic work to-day so admired by all, whether native or foreign, who know the Russian language.

During his lifetime, he changed his style several times, and each time he added new qualities which made his verse the more inimitable. In his early years, when he was still under the influence of Byron, as in the Fountain of Bakhchisaray, he developed to the highest degree the exotic and sensuous properties of the Russian language. Then as he matured still more, his style became much less adorned. He omitted all superfluous words and, in the bareness of his language, he created a strange dignity which is even more inimitable than his earlier exotic and ornate poems. Perhaps no one has ever expressed in simple words such grandeur and such dignity. I say, in simple words, for there are whole stanzas of Poushkin which seem devoid of any attempt to rise to poetic heights. The vocabulary seems to be that of prose or even of colloquial speech, and yet it requires no prejudice or partisanship to discover that in these stanzas there exists a something which stamps them as real poetry, written with a surprising economy of means.

Here is to be found one of the great merits of Poushkin. When we compare his language with the ponderous and often grandiloquent, if not bathistic, work of the eighteenth century, we realize that, during his short life, he actually created a new literary language. He took the best elements that existed in the Russian language, and in colloquial speech, and fused them into a new medium of expression available for writers to come, and which has been the basis of all good Russian literature from that day to this.

Another striking quality in Poushkin's art, is his surprising balance and common sense. Poushkin inherited to the full an appreciation of all that Russia had acquired in the eighteenth century. It was a period when the court at St. Petersburg en-

THE RENAISSANCE 21

deavored to assimilate, with characteristic Russian vitality, the pseudo-classic art of France. This is apparent in every form of her art, architecture, painting, drama, and poetry of every kind. Much of this work is crude, bombastic, and conceited, but there is, in all of it, a definite strain of accomplishment and discipline which binds within its rigid forms the often unbridled energy of the Russian people. Poushkin felt this strongly, and if we examine his work from this point of view, we shall see that perhaps he alone of all the Russian writers really understood and appreciated the self-restraint of French art.

Even with this understanding and appreciation, he never lost sight of, or failed to appreciate, the more robust forms of native development. He was able to understand a Peter the Great; he was able to comprehend the nature of the explosion that took place in the uprising of Pougachev; he was able to appreciate the career of Boris Godounov, and, above all, he was able to represent in artistic form the legends of the people, as found in their series of poetic tales, such as the Golden Cock, Czar Saltan, and The Fisherman and the Fish.*

Thus it is fair to say that, by the time Poushkin made his first appearance in the literary field, he had a complete understanding of the Russian peo-

* "The Russian Wonderland"—a Metrical Translation by Boris Brasol; The Paisley Press, 1936.

ple and of the little which existed, in the way of Russian literature. He was recognized almost at once as the master of the entire period, and he did not need to suffer death before this palm was awarded him.

His attitude toward the society of his own day, as seen in Eugene Onegin, is equally masterly. It is true that he commenced this poem-novel on the model of Byron's Don Juan, but with his magic pen, he escaped from the influence of the foreigner, and produced a novel, where, for the first time, real characters of his own day and class of society moved upon the stage. It has been well said that Tatyana is, perhaps, the first heroine of the type that was later made famous by Turgenev, and that Eugene himself is the ancestor of all the disillusioned and repentant noblemen, striving to escape from a reality which they will not master, to a better world somewhere else; and who cast a despondent shadow over all of subsequent Russian literature, giving to the world an appreciation of the Russian character which is founded neither on personal experience, nor on historical reality.

Yet in saying this, we are really emphasizing the superiority of Poushkin over all of his successors, for his sense of proportion and his sense of balance did not lead him to magnify the Onegins, out of all proportion to other types of Russian life. He realized that the Russian nature was not so one-sided, that there were many inter-

THE RENAISSANCE 23

ests in the life of the Russian people, and that it was impossible to compress into one narrow formula the life of all the people of a great empire. Let us consider the geographic range of his subjects. We shall find him writing about the two capitals, St. Petersburg and Moscow. He goes down to the Black Sea and the Caucasus. He touches the steppes of southeastern Russia and the plains of the Ukraine and of Bessarabia. He writes not merely of Russians, but of Tatars, Gypsies, and the mixed races bordering on the Black Sea. Few of the authors who succeeded him ranged so far and wide. Perhaps they travelled more extensively abroad, for Poushkin was never outside of the boundaries of his own land, but he was not one of those who confined their vision to the two Russian capitals, to Paris, and to Rome, and thought that they knew the world. He wrote about Russia, and, under his pen, Russia was not perhaps a heaven, but it was not a mere hell on earth.

He appreciated the good and the bad sides of his own country. In his epigrams he chastised mercilessly many of the prominent figures of the day. He spoke plainly of the cruel oppression of the tribesmen, in the story of Pougachev. He emphasized the poverty of the urban population, in the Copper Horseman. Yet at the same time he did not seek to remedy these evils by advocating the destruction of the Russian Empire. At the time of the Polish revolt of 1831, he turned against his old friend, the Pole Mickiewicz, and defied Europe to repeat Napoleon's attempt, and meet his fate. He carried this note of patriotism even into his poems on the anniversaries of the Lycée where he had been educated, and showed, throughout, a balance between a spirit of absolute condemnation and one of undignified laudation of the ruling powers.

To these outstanding qualities we can add still another, rarely to be found in his successors—the gift of handling serious things in a light way. Tolstoy was conspicuously lacking in this gift. We need only look at the heavy handed irony with which he sketches the lifelessness of Karenin, or the ruthless way in which he unmasks society, to feel the difference between his touch and that of Pushkin. The one is intent upon a moral mission which brooks no delay. The other, with an apparent neglect of the question at hand, drops a single phrase, which reveals the entire situation far more clearly than do the serious statements of the other. Take in Eugene Onegin such remarks as "Her father saw no harm in books, although he never read any"; these few words, expressed in Poushkin's best and lightest manner, throw into prominence the lack of interest in literature on the part of many of the provincial landowners of his day, far better than any diatribe on the benighted character of the provinces as pæaned by a modern reformer.

THE RENAISSANCE 25

This lightness and apparent frivolity were an outstanding characteristic of Poushkin in life as well as in art, and won him the nickname of "the Cricket." He was always interested in some new thing. He was always playing for some new affection, some new interest, and it led many of his more serious friends and comrades to doubt his sincerity, his wisdom, and his tact. Perhaps it was this very quality that kept him from being more seriously involved in the Decembrist conspiracy, when the leaders of his social and intellectual group started the noblest and the most futile of all of Russia's revolutionary movements, for no one realized what was to be even the second step in an endeavor to overthrow the established order.

Finally we must remember that Poushkin belonged to the old aristocracy of Russia. He was not of a super-rich or superancient family, but he was proud that his ancestors played a rôle, two hundred and fifty years before his time, in the reign of Ivan the Terrible. He was proud that through his grandfather Hannibal, he was in close touch with Peter the Great, and that he had the privilege of being received in society. He was a graduate of the Lyceum of Czarskoe Selo, which was attended by the sons of the noblest and the most prominent families, and he moved during his entire life amid the great, the prominent, and the famous. This undoubtedly had an influence on his life and work.

We may not go so far as to say that he preferred ancestry to merit, although perhaps he showed it in accepting a post at court under Nicholas I; but he did stand out as one of the gentleman writers—should we to-day call them amateurs, and compare them with the amateur tennis and polo-players, who perhaps spend more time upon their game than do any professionals? In this respect Poushkin was nearing the end of a period, for after the death of the poet Lermontov, only four years later than his own, the control of literature passed definitely into the hands of men who had broken away from the social life of the Empire and its official existence, or who had never had a place within that charmed circle. In this again, Poushkin was typical of the eighteenth century, when all the writers were recognized not for their literary merit but for their social status, and when the returns which marked literary success were expressed in the same careers and honors that marked political or military fame.

It was to this circumstance, perhaps more than any other, that Poushkin owed his neglect abroad. The last decade of his life was occupied with a constant series of conflicts and unpleasantnesses with the rising professional writers. The enthusiastic groups of gentleman authors were coming to an end. Poushkin missed them and their advice and criticism. On the other hand, upstarts such as Bulgarin were attacking him with a sort of inverse snobbery, for they believed, or affected to believe, that any author who could be received at court or who was interested in being there, must be ipso facto deficient in talent, in ability, in self-respect, and in pride. The last years of Poushkin's life were filled with attacks of this nature, and these attacks became still more bitter after his untimely death. It is not without significance that the great critic Belinsky, the apostle of the entire school of sociological criticism, never wrote a thorough and mature criticism on Poushkin, and the word of Belinsky was the fundamental law of Russian literary criticism until the nineties. The situation was still worse in later decades, when Pisarev proudly declared that, for the welfare of the nation, boots were greater than Poushkin. In fact during the forty years that followed the death of Poushkin, it was almost taboo to read poetry of any kind, or to comment on any piece of literature which did not have a distinct social value. To save the few last shreds of Poushkin's reputation, the liberals of the day read through his works, hoping against hope to find passages which would serve to prove that he was really radical, even as to-day, and in his own day, friends searched to prove that he was conservative. It is all so similar to the ponderous volumes written to prove that Shakespeare was a Catholic or a Protestant, that he was or was not a poacher at Stratford-on-Avon. But it was not until

Dostoyevsky boldly and decisively lashed out at the critics of all sides in his Poushkin speech delivered in Moscow in 1880, that the Russians themselves began to evaluate or take an interest in Poushkin. They had read him before, but now they dared to be proud of him, and it was only then that they began to study his writings and to endeavor to learn the secrets of his art.

The damage to Poushkin's reputation abroad was already done. In the meantime Russian literature had penetrated Europe. Turgenev, Tolstoy, and Dostoyevsky were becoming known, and Russian literature was already being read for its negative qualities and for its ideas of futility. The healthy character of Poushkin did not seem Russian. The emigrées of those days were largely in the political opposition, and they repeated abroad the senseless patter of the preceding decades, when Poushkin was being neglected. Hence the influence of Poushkin abroad was blocked at every turn. To the Russian emigrées of the day, he was a mere sycophant and courtier; to the people abroad, he was not a Russian, as they wished to know Russians.

Hence it has been a long struggle to bring home to the people of Europe and America the real significance of Poushkin. He is almost untranslatable, and the few products of his pen that have come abroad, are frequently unworthy of the master. Hence also the very strange phenomenon that many of the best translations of Poushkin in English were those of his own lifetime, when visitors to Russia felt the inspiration and the grandeur of the poet and his times. From 1840 to the beginning of the twentieth century, there are few translations that are worthwhile. Perhaps there have not been many good ones since, for translations of a genius are usually unsatisfactory, and there are few geniuses engaged in the work of translation!

However that may be, it is now one hundred years since the death of Alexander Sergeyevich Poushkin. His fame at home, despite revolts and revolutions, is growing greater and greater. He is being recognized as a figure who in manysidedness, in balance, in artistic composition, stands alone in the whole field of Russian literature, its fountain-head, its first master, and its greatest expositor. We can only hope that the world abroad, during the second century after his death, will come to understand and to appreciate him, and to give him his proper place among the great masters of world literature, as the poet of Russia and the Russian people.

IV

ALEXANDER SERGEYEVITCH PUSHKIN

A Biographical Sketch by
PETER MALEVSKY-MALEVITCH

BOYHOOD

BORN in Moscow on May 26, 1799,* Alexander Sergeyevitch Pushkin belonged on his father's side to one of the oldest Moscow families "with a six century old historical record." None of his paternal ancestors were men of great note, but they were all well educated and men of means. On his mother's side, his great grandfather was Count Ibrahim (Abraham) Petrovitch Gannibal (Hannibal), the celebrated "Arab of Peter the Great," son of an Ethiopian chieftain, probably of Amharic blood. Gannibal, a hostage at the court of the Sultan of Turkey, was bought or stolen by the emissaries of the Czar, who caused him to receive a brilliant education, and subsequently gave him the daughter of one of his courtiers in marriage. Later Peter the Great made him Brigadier General of Engineers, and a Count of the Russian

* Old style Russian calendar used throughout this sketch.

A BIOGRAPHICAL SKETCH 31

Empire. Pushkin was fond of attributing the tempestuous and passionate side of his nature to his African blood; and certainly his descent was evident in the thick lips, swarthy complexion, and abundant curly hair shown in the portraits that have come down to us.

Pushkin's parents were pleasure loving, extravagant, and impoverished members of the nobility, remarkable in no sense. His father could claim a certain superficial culture and some knowledge of foreign languages (chiefly French), and affected an interest in philosophy, literature, and the arts, in accordance with traditions dating back to the "golden age of Catherine the Great."

At this time French was the recognized language of educated Russians, and accordingly Pushkin spoke and read this language in childhood. By the time he was ten, he had had several French tutors, and under their influence read, in his father's library, Voltaire, Rousseau, Molière, Parny, Grécourt, and many other of the frivolous, erotic, and now forgotten French Eighteenth Century writers.

In the absence of any real intimacy between him and his parents, the boy was left principally to the influence of his maternal grandmother and his nurse, Arina Rodionovna. Of the two, his nurse was much more important, since from her he learned not only the Russian language, but much of Russian folklore. At this time Russian was the language of the vulgar and peasants; and was still waiting for someone to raise it as a literary language to the level of a great cultural force. The gift of a literary language to his country was subsequently perhaps the greatest task that Pushkin achieved, and his achievement was due primarily to the early influence of his peasant nurse. Some credit for his literary inclination must also be given to his paternal uncle, Vasily Lvovitch, a minor poet of some note, who was largely responsible for bringing to the Pushkin home such contemporary giants of Russian literature as Karamzin, Joukovsky, Viazemsky, and Batiushkov.

Under these influences Pushkin wrote, before he was twelve, two French comedies and a number of lyric verses, none of which have survived. They sufficed to bring the boy's gifts to the attention of Karamzin and Joukovsky, who accepted the boy, even at this early age, as an apprentice to their company of poets. Between these associations, and his contacts with Russian country life, folklore and customs at his grandmother's suburban estate, Pushkin's inquisitive, sensitive and precocious mind absorbed a wealth of impressions, which were later to be recorded in the most exquisite verse and prose ever written in his native tongue.

STUDENT YEARS

Through the kind offices of a family friend, A. I. Turgenev, Pushkin was entered, in 1811, at the age of twelve, in the Lyceum newly created by Tsar Alexander I in Tsarkoye Selo, near St. Petersburg. A new departure in Russian education, it followed the ideas of the Emperor's Swiss tutor, La Harpe, and of Count M. M. Speransky, both liberal minded and highly educated men.

Quarters were allotted to the Lyceum in the Tsar's palace, and it was dedicated to the education of young nobles for the service of the state "in a spirit of liberalism, integrity, and achievement," with the motto written by the Emperor himself "For the common weal."

Pushkin was a member of the first class to enter and to graduate from the Lyceum. The curriculum, combining in those six years both secondary and university education, was left intentionally free from professional studies. The first three years were devoted principally to Latin, Russian and French literature, rhetoric, and natural history. The three senior years included law, political economy, philosophy, and advanced literature. The students were taught rather the method of learning a subject than the subject itself, and the course was in general a liberal but rather worldly education. While it must be admitted that the knowledge of the graduates was superficial, they were at least equipped with a broad outlook, the genuine love of knowledge, and both inclination and ability to continue acquiring it in after life. The considerable number of alumni, distinguished in statesmanship, art, and science, was the best justification of the institution.

The distinguished faculty included Koshansky, Professor of Rhetoric and Russian Literature, Kunitzyn, Professor of Public Law, Galitch, in philosophy, and Malinovsky and Engelhardt, in general leadership. Discipline was lenient, corporal punishment excluded, and self government encouraged. Living accommodations were private and comfortable. Friendship among the students was encouraged and, under the leadership of Pushkin's class, was handed down as a tradition of the institution. This tradition of friendship became so integral a part of the poet's maturity, as to permeate all his writing. An analysis of his literary vocabulary proves the point beyond peradventure. In Eugene Onegin alone there are more references to the relation of friendship than any other subject except love. Much the same is true of the large number of Pushkin's so-called Lyceum poems, not to mention the frequent poetic epistles addressed specifically to various friends.

School magazines, choirs, and theatrical and literary associations flourished at the Lyceum under faculty encouragement. In these activities the leaders included Pushkin himself, then nicknamed

A BIOGRAPHICAL SKETCH 35

the "Frenchman" and also the "Cricket," and his life long friends, Yakovlev, later a dilettante composer, Pushchin, a coming jurist, Küchelbecker, poet and critic, Prince Gortchakov, later Chancellor and Minister of Foreign Affairs, Baron Antony Delvig, a poet of undoubted brilliance and Pushkin's closest friend through life.

Neither studious nor diligent, Pushkin excelled in rhetoric, philosophy, and literature. Restless, undisciplined, lazy, he yet read voraciously, was a brilliant linguist, and developed a colossal memory. He was early acknowledged by his classmates and teachers as a leader, particularly in literary and theatrical activities. Often irritable, quarrelsome, tactless, he alternated between great sweetness and shyness of temperament, and fits of despondency and self-depreciation. Despite his many faults, his intimates were devoted to him, and throughout his school days Pushkin breathed an atmosphere of friendship and admiration. His Lyceum years were without doubt the happiest of his life; and his personality and character blossomed in this sympathetic atmosphere.

It is well to remember that these school years were also years of great historical importance. 1812 was marked by the French invasion, the burning of Moscow, and Napoleon's historic and disastrous retreat. 1813 saw the liberation of Germany by the Russians, and 1814 the fall of Napoleon, followed by the ascendency in all Europe of Tsar Alexander. Finally, 1815 included the Hundred Days, Waterloo, and the final eclipse of Napoleon. These great events visibly influenced the budding genius of Pushkin, recognized not only by his schoolmates, but by the leading literary figures of the day. As early as 1814, his ode, "To a Poet Friend," was published in a leading literary magazine, and the following year he publicly recited before a brilliant gathering his later ode, "Memories of Tsarskoe Selo." It was on this occasion that the "patriarch of the Russian Muses," Derzhavin, "jumped up, embraced our young poet, and with tears in his eyes, gave him his blessing; we all were spellbound and sat in reverent silence" (Pushchin).

Thus, at fifteen, Pushkin had already achieved reputation, the salons were open to him, and his company was sought by the leaders of literature, society, and the army. Encouraged by recognition, he wrote steadily and, on graduation, at the age of eighteen, had already accumulated a large book of verses.

EARLY MANHOOD

Appointed an attaché at the Foreign Office after graduation, Pushkin was accepted in society, at eighteen, as a fully grown man. At once he established a reputation for worldliness and amorous adventure among the numerous ladies of easy virtue of the period. His name, his talents, his wit, his

A BIOGRAPHICAL SKETCH 37

excellent manners, and his accomplished French, all made him a welcome guest in St. Petersburg society.

The Imperial city and the Russian court of the time, characterized by extraordinary brilliancy, were the center of European political and artistic pilgrimage. The social season was a succession of brilliant receptions, the theatre flourished, young bloods vied for the favors of the belles of the stage, and spent their time in orgies of pleasurable excitement. "The Cricket," in the words of A. I. Turgenev, "dances his feet off on the boulevards, does not sleep nights, pays court even to the ticket girls at the theatres, and is completely out of hand." Through all these associations, Pushkin acquired an intimate acquaintance with, and love for the society of St. Petersburg. He became its poet *par excellence,* and, among the many friends acquired at the time, prepared the way for his later dangerous involvement with the Decembrist revolt of 1825. At the same time they confirmed his dangerous tendency to the waste of his time and substance in extravagant dissipation. This in turn intensified his bad relations with his father, who was as stingy as he was profligate. The older man was inclined to resent his son's promiscuous and expensive love affairs, as well as his continuous addiction to drunkenness, gambling, and duelling.

This period in Pushkin's life is adequately summed in a description by his schoolfellow,

Korff, "He indulged in debauchery of every kind, passing days and nights in constant succession of bacchanalian revels and orgies."

Undeterred by any religious belief or moral code, led on by his youth and by the spirit of the time when wine, women, gambling and duelling were the fashion, Pushkin's life and tendencies were as natural as they were perhaps in some respects unfortunate.

On the literary side, Pushkin at this time joined the so-called younger school of the literati in a club, Arzamas, founded by the historian, Karamzin, and headed by the poet, Joukovsky. The club was liberal in its artistic ideas, cosmopolitan, and mildly atheistic. Standing for the modernization of Russian life and language, the Arzamas society showed definite liberal leanings, and included a number of younger revolutionaries. Pushkin's membership had a much more lasting effect on him than his social escapades. It helped him to realize the need for developing and perfecting his talent. He set vigorously at the task of completing his education, read copiously, and devoted himself seriously to the study of the drama in French, English, and German.

At this time also he established friendly relations with a number of outstanding men of the time, among them Colonel Kaverin, of the Preobrazhensky Guards, a remarkable poet and excellent critic. Perhaps through him Pushkin also

A BIOGRAPHICAL SKETCH 39

acquired the friendship of Captain Chaadaev of the Hussars, a philosopher of independent and austere thought. At the same time he became increasingly intimate with Karamzin, who, though nominally a member of the Arzamas society, was really a mild conservative, a profound Christian, and always in the good graces of the authorities. It was due to him that Pushkin, the radical of 1818, gradually became the patriot and nationalist of 1830. An equally excellent influence was that of Joukovsky, a poet of the greatest merit, who, in conjunction with Karamzin, was at a later period of the greatest assistance to Pushkin in his continual difficulties with the powers that were.

While during all these years Pushkin displayed continuous creative activity, it was not until 1820 that he published the first work on which his subsequent fame can be said to rest, "Ruslan and Ludmila." On the occasion of this publication, Joukovsky congratulated him with a dedication of a portrait "To a victorious pupil from a defeated master."

Among the great number of verses which he also wrote at the time, "Freedom," in which the assassination of Paul I was exalted as a warning to tyrants, unfortunately reached, in manuscript form, the Emperor Alexander, and touched him closely, as his participation in the plot to dethrone his father had brought him near to both patricide and regicide. In consequence of this and other revolutionary poems, the Tsar inclined to make an example of Pushkin by banishing him to the monastery of Solovki on the White Sea "to think over and repent of his disgusting writings." Through the intervention of Karamzin and Joukovsky, the sentence was mitigated to banishment to Southern Russia, under the guise of a minor clerkship in the "Board of Protection of Foreign Colonists." Accordingly Pushkin left St. Petersburg on May 6, 1820, southward bound.

Pushkin's actual politics have been the cause of much argument. Actually Pushkin was fundamentally uninterested in the politics of the day, and never showed any aptitude for political activity. His occasional incendiary poems rather reflected the opinions of his friends than any rooted convictions of his own. His love of freedom and his hatred of oppression, like his passion for beauty, were general rather than particular. In no sense was he ever actually a conspirator or an active revolutionary. Nevertheless, the government, both under Alexander I and later under Nicholas I, could hardly be expected to overlook such irritants as Pushkin's revolutionary verses. On the other hand, it may well be that the various penalties inflicted on him were rather a stimulus to his work than a deterrent. In any event, he resented the Tsar's censorship almost entirely from the point of view of a literary curb. At no time was

Pushkin's concrete interest in politics sufficiently keen or concrete, to cut much of a figure in his career.

EXILE

Irritated at his banishment in the midst of a hectic love affair with a lady impossible now to identify, Pushkin duly reported to his new chief, General I. M. Inzov, Viceroy of Bessarabia at Ekaterinoslav, who, from their first meeting, became the poet's friend and protector. When Pushkin fell seriously ill with a malign fever, the General kindly sanctioned a leave of absence so that he might receive the care of his friend, Raevsky, son of the celebrated General and hero of the war of 1812, who fortunately turned up at this juncture in his father's company. After a short stay at Piatigorsk, where Pushkin was much benefited by the mineral baths, the party travelled along the River Taman, which then divided Russian territory from the hostile mountaineers of the Caucasus. The magnificent scenery, the almost legendary stories of the struggles between Russians and Circassians, were commemorated in the famous poem "Prisoner of the Caucasus."

A subsequent delightful stay on the estate of the Raevsky's at Gurzuf, with the charm of cultivated feminine society, completely restored Pushkin's health and spirits. Later travels with the same family in the Crimea were signalized in due course by the admirable poem, "The Fountain of Bakhchissarai."

During Pushkin's absence, General Inzov had been transferred to Kishinev, capital of Bessarabia, and it was to that semi-Asiatic city that Pushkin returned. In the absence of specific duties of consequence, he spent several months, during the winter of 1820/21, at the estate of V. L. Davidov, a half brother of General Raevsky; and here made the acquaintance of a number of leaders of the later Decembrist conspiracy. Pushkin was, however, far more interested in flirtation, love intrigue, and general discussion, than in politics. In the late winter, he was obliged to go to Kishinev, where he was profoundly unhappy; and in 1823 wrote of it—"accursed town of Kishinev, of abusing you the tongue will never grow tired." Kishinev had been annexed from Turkey only a few years before, and was still a dirty, sprawling village, populated by a mixture of Moldavians, Greeks, Jews, and Bulgarians, with a very limited number of Russian officials. With such small opportunity for pleasant associations, and merely negligible duties, Pushkin soon reverted to his former life of indiscriminate love affairs, carousing and gambling. At the same time he found much leisure both for writing and study, and his limited salary, even with the help of occasional substantial sums from publishers, acted as an effective restraint on his dissipation.

At the recommendation of his chief, General Inzov, he was presently transferred to the Chancellery of Count M. Vorontzow, at Odessa. This at least was a return to civilization with much pleasanter associations, even though with less fortunate official contacts.

His stay in Odessa was notable for two simultaneous love affairs, one with the beautiful and completely amoral wife of a Dalmatian merchant, Amalia Riznitch, the other with the wife of his chief, Countess Elizabeth Vorontzov. Perhaps the latter affair, though platonic, was somewhat responsible for Pushkin's strained relations with the Count, which finally culminated in the poet's removal from the service, and exile to his family's estate, Mikhailovskoe, in the Province of Pskov (1824). While the circumstances of his lonely exile were unpleasant, they resulted in the greatest literary production of any period in Pushkin's life, including a considerable number of his longer and more important poems, as well as "Eugene Onegin."

When Pushkin first came to Mikhailovskoe, his family was in residence, and a permanent bitterness was created by the attempts of his father to act at once as spy and jailer. The result was a scene of physical violence, almost resulting in the jailing of the poet. The only happy consequence was that the family departed and left Pushkin to himself, with only the company of his old nurse, Arina.

From now on the poet's life became one of work and study, particularly of Russian and foreign classics, including the works of Shakespeare. His loneliness was occasionally alleviated by visits from his old school friends, Delvig, Pushchin, and Gorchakov.

The only neighbors whose society Pushkin could frequent with pleasure, were Madame P. A. Osipov and her children. During the summer of 1825, Madame Osipov entertained her niece, Madame Kern, with whom Pushkin promptly fell in love, and addressed to her one of his loveliest poems "I Remember a Wonderful Moment." Pushkin's letters to her after her departure, form his only extant correspondence with any of his mistresses.

In addition to his writings for publication, a further insight into his intellectual development in exile is attainable from the fact that he enlivened his leisure with a plentiful correspondence with many of his friends.

FREEDOM

On November 19, 1825, Tsar Alexander I died, and the news of his death brought new hope of return from exile to our poet. Unknown to the public, the next in line to the throne, the late Tsar having been childless, Grand Duke Constantine, had abdicated in favor of his younger brother, Grand Duke Nicholas. Without knowledge of this abdication, a movement in favor of the succession of Grand Duke Constantine as against Nicholas culminated in the Decembrist revolt, which being badly organized and managed, was quickly suppressed. As a consequence, many of Pushkin's closest friends were condemned to death or exile in Siberia, and through his friendships with the conspirators, Pushkin himself was suspected of a part in the revolt, though it was later proved that he had known practically nothing about it in advance.

At last, in September, 1826, he received a summons to report to the Tsar in person, at Moscow. The audience lasted over an hour, and resulted apparently in mutual admiration on the part of the protagonists. The Tsar pardoned the poet unconditionally, gave him leave to settle where he wished, travel and write at his pleasure. While exempted from the general censorship, Pushkin was to be subject to the personal censorship of the Tsar, to which he was to conform by sending all his writings, prior to publication, to the head of His Majesty's Private Chancellery, Count Benkendorff, for inspection and transmission to the Tsar. This proved in reality a severer measure than the general censorship, and irked the poet vastly for the ensuing years, until his early and tragic death. The severity of the measure is proved by the single incident of Pushkin's venturing to read his yet unpublished tragedy of "Boris Godounov" to a circle of friends, a few weeks after the interview with the Tsar, referred to above. The result was a severe rebuke, and proof of the Tsar's displeasure took the form of refusing to the poet permission to publish the tragedy for the ensuing five years.

In spite of such restraints, the newly acquired "freedom" went like wine to Pushkin's head. He became once more the favorite of society and of his comrades in literature. The year of 1827 saw him at the height of his popularity. He was involved in innumerable love affairs: Madame Kern, the Countess Zakrevskaya, and many others succeeded each other at brief intervals, and shared his love with many less distinguished women. In fact he returned altogether to his old round of gambling, carousing, and flirtation.

In 1828, there began a literary reaction in which Pushkin, under the attacks of the advanced young writers of the day, gradually became the leader of the conservative and aristocratic wing in literature. From that time on, he was the victim of a bitter campaign of abuse from the more radical journals, such as The Moscow Messenger.

He became at last weary of the dissolute life which he had led for years, and felt the urge to establish a home of his own. In 1829, he fell desperately in love with Natalie Gontcharov, a young woman of exceptional beauty, belonging to the lesser nobility. Hereafter there were to be few additions to the famous "Don Juan" list of some

A BIOGRAPHICAL SKETCH

thirty-seven ladies with whom he had had amorous relations, which he sent to one of his correspondents. Incidentally, the word ladies is here used advisedly, since he included in the list none of the demi-mondaines with whom he had consorted.

Pushkin's suit was rejected by the lady's mother; in consequence of which Pushkin, in despair, and without asking for leave of absence, decamped to the Caucasus to join the army fighting the Turks, under Field Marshal Paskevitch in that region. He was well received by the General, under Benkendorff's instructions, and accompanied the army to Erzeroum, participating with an almost childish pleasure in several minor engagements. By the middle of September, he was back in Moscow, having produced a considerable number of verses, and his "Journey to Erzeroum."

The trip, however, involved him in further difficulties with Benkendorff and the Tsar, serving to remind him of the constant shackles upon his apparent freedom.

MARRIAGE

The last months of Pushkin's bachelorhood were perhaps the most unhappy and despondent period of his life, as witnessed by his correspondence. His feelings were further exasperated by continual refusals of his requests to travel abroad in search of forgetfulness. At last, however, his friend, Delvig, succeeded in distracting him by offering him an editorial position on a new and strictly non-political journal—The Literary Gazette. This at least gave Pushkin the long awaited opportunity to hit back at the critics who had been annoying him like veritable gadflies. He started a crusade in favor of art for art's sake, and made the fullest use of his opportunities to belabor his opponents. Until the suppression of The Literary Gazette in 1831, it gave the poet a renewed interest in life, helped to restore peace to his troubled spirit, and so incidentally revived his matrimonial hopes.

In the spring of 1830, he again proposed to Natalie, and this time obtained her mother's conditional consent. One of the conditions was an assurance from government that Pushkin was once more persona grata; and this assurance Pushkin was finally able to obtain. He obtained, in addition, certain financial favors from the government for the impoverished Gontcharovs, as well as permission for himself to publish at long last "Boris Godounov," which brought him a sufficient financial honorarium to make his marriage possible. At the same time a formal reconciliation with his family resulted in the gift from his father of the estate of Boldino, in the Province of Nizhni Novgorod.

During a visit to take possession of Boldino,

accidentally prolonged because of a cholera epidemic, Pushkin achieved a greater production within a few months than at almost any other time in his life. He finished at this place "Eugene Onegin," wrote "The Tales of Belkin," "The Little House in Kolomna," and a considerable series of admirable lyrics.

At about this time, also, he had produced the four admirable one-act plays in verse—"Mozart and Salieri," "The Feast During the Plague," "The Covetous Knight" and "The Stone Guest"—as well as "The History of the Manor of Goriukhino."

The following year began very sadly for Pushkin with the death, on January 14th, of his life long friend, Delvig; and served to dampen his joy at the approaching solemnization of his wedding on February 18th.

Pushkin's marriage has been a highly controversial topic in the hands of his biographers. Some have represented his wife as his evil genius, who, by her complete lack of sympathy, combined with senseless extravagance, dragged his spirit into the mire. Others have represented her as the victim of an over-jealous, over sensual, and utterly self-centered genius who never understood her. The truth is simply that the two were utterly unsuited.

Pushkin's love for Natalie was extraordinarily deep and sincere. On the other hand, he expressed very grave doubts in advance whether happiness could be possible in the face of so great a disparity of years and of background.

For Natalie, her marriage was primarily an escape from bondage, and a rise from straitened circumstances, into the glitter and enchantment of the court. She had nothing to offer the poet beyond her brilliant beauty, and her scarcely assailable virtue. Her mind was superficial, she was not interested in Pushkin's work or in his literary friends, she was not even a competent housewife; and being incompetent, was necessarily extravagant. This extravagance, however, went beyond mere incompetence. Natalie craved luxury, was indifferent to money, and seems to have felt she was entitled to spend it freely, while it was her husband's part to foot the bills by borrowing, begging from the Tsar, or working harder to obtain the needed funds.

The young couple settled first in Tsarskoe Selo, where Madame Pushkin was presented at court, and made a strong impression on the Emperor. Subsequently they moved to St. Petersburg to a house not far from the winter palace—a house that shortly became a rendezvous for all that was fashionable in society. It was a world to which Pushkin was accustomed since birth, but to him now totally unsympathetic. Moreover, the influx of admirers frequently awakened his jealousy. On the other hand, his own friends found little favor in his wife's eyes, nor she in theirs. The result was

A BIOGRAPHICAL SKETCH 51

that Pushkin could find relaxation only away from his own home in such salons as were sympathetic to him. He failed utterly to adapt himself to the butterfly existence that his wife enjoyed, just as he failed to interest her in his own views and diversions. There seemed no middle way for partners each incapable of compromise.

Moreover, the couple were living far beyond their means. Natalie was a "help only at squandering, and a worker only with her feet at balls" complained Pushkin in one of his letters.

Obsession with financial difficulties not only made Pushkin irritable, but caused him to become grasping and intractable with his publishers, and to make futile efforts at increasing his income by entering into the commercial side of publishing. Despite all this, his debts grew steadily and forced him into the hands of usurers. On several occasions appeals to the Emperor brought generous relief, but never permanently cured the poet's difficulties.

It was partly his financial difficulties that caused him to apply for a government grant to write a history of the Pougachev Rebellion. Perhaps also the prospect of escape from a life he detested, in leaving St. Petersburg to visit the field of rebellion, had its share in forwarding the project. Its utility, from the literary point of view, was relatively small, as the circumstances inhibited Pushkin from expressing himself freely in this historical work. It had, however, one fortunate consequence in that it gave him the material for one of his most admirable works of fiction—"The Captain's Daughter."

By 1834, his pecuniary difficulties and growing disgust with the emptiness of his existence, persuaded Pushkin that the way to salvation lay in retirement from the capital to his country estate. The project excited a storm of protest on his wife's part; and it is not impossible that she may have appealed directly, or indirectly through her friends, to the Emperor himself. In any event, when Pushkin applied, in 1835, for permission to retire to Boldino for two years, the request was refused on the ground that, as a member of the civil service, he was not entitled to so long a leave. For a person whose official position was purely honorary, the excuse seems thin. In any event, it convinced Pushkin that his bonds were real, and that from them there was no escape. It may be, however, that a following grant from the Tsar of 30,000 rubles to pay his more pressing personal debts, may have somewhat served to soften the blow.

In the next year, despite numerous previous refusals, Pushkin at last received permission to publish a quarterly magazine—The Contemporary. After only four issues, it came to an end with Pushkin's death; and it was never profitable in a business way. During its short life, however, it was remarkable for its literary quality and the eminence of its list of contributors, which included, besides Pushkin, Joukovsky, Gogol, Tutchev, and others of almost equal standing. Pushkin devoted himself wholeheartedly to the magazine while it lasted, but its lack of success was too conspicuous to allow it to afford him much gratification. He was tired and restless, weary of the life he led, dreaming of liberty and peace. All these feelings found ample expression in the lyrics of his last years, which are full also of the theme of death, and forebodings of tragedy.

DEATH

Outwardly the poet's home life seemed normal enough. Three children were born of his marriage, and in them the poet took great delight. Husband and wife appeared everywhere together, and seemed to share the same pursuits and pleasures. Moreover, after the two unmarried sisters of Natalie came to live with them in 1834, the poet found an intimate and devoted friend in his sister-in-law, Alexandra. Nevertheless, the relations between husband and wife were marked with increasing tension. Pushkin complained frequently of her growing coldness and pre-occupation with various young men in society. His jealousy continually increased, and led him at times to the verge of absurdity.

Prominent among Natalie's admirers was the

Baron d'Anthès, a Frenchman adopted as a son by the Dutch Minister, Baron de Heeckeren. The young Baron was admitted to the Chevalier Gardes, and soon became a prominent member of St. Petersburg society. Handsome, well educated, an excellent and indefatigable dancer, he was also an unscrupulous intriguer and Don Juan.

His conspicuous and almost compromising attentions to Natalie, in 1836, filled the air with unpleasant rumors. Finally Pushkin received a letter in the name of the "Illustrious Order of Cuckolds," electing him to the position of historian of the order. Dozens of copies of the letter were also sent to Pushkin's friends.

Pushkin without any special evidence, leapt to the conclusion that the letter emanated from Baron de Heeckeren, and in response sent a challenge to d'Anthès. The duel was averted by the extraordinary expedient of persuading d'Anthès to write Pushkin that his frequent presence at the poet's house was dictated by his love for Natalie's sister, Catherine, whom he desired to marry. Pushkin, while in no position to forbid the marriage, refused to see d'Anthès, and forbade Natalie to see him. d'Anthès and Catherine Gontcharov were actually married on January 10, 1837.

The marriage, instead of mending matters, made them worse. It gave Natalie frequent colorable pretexts for meeting her new brother-in-law. When this came to Pushkin's ears he wrote, on

A BIOGRAPHICAL SKETCH 55

January 26, 1837, the most insulting letter to the old Baron de Heeckeren, accusing him of being a procurer for his adopted son. In response, d'Anthès challenged Pushkin to a duel, and Pushkin not only accepted, but kept the matter secret to prevent interference.

Pushkin's actions in the matter of the duel must be considered in the light of his complete dissatisfaction with the life he was leading, rather than from the point of view of mere jealousy. No doubt he hoped that the duel and the inevitable scandal would cut for him the Gordian knot, and compel his retirement from society into the country. There is no evidence that he thought his wife guilty of anything worse than frivolity and imprudence.

The duel was fixed for four in the afternoon on January 27. Pushkin's second was an old school fellow, Danzas. All of the morning and early afternoon, the poet spent writing letters, which showed no traces of undue emotion. He even wrote a literary aspirant that he had perused her book that day, and had admired her style.

Driving to the scene of the duel, Pushkin and his second passed and greeted many acquaintances. Madame Pushkin returning from a drive, failed to see her husband through her nearsightedness, but he saw her.

Duly arrived at the appointed place, Pushkin showed great impatience at the lengthy preliminaries dictated by the Code. At last, the signal being given, d'Anthès fired first, and Pushkin fell, wounded in the abdomen. He motioned away the second, saying "Je me sens assez de force pour donner mon coup." Firing in his turn, he slightly wounded d'Anthès. Pushkin refused a reconciliation, saying "If I recover, we will have to go over it again." He was losing much blood, and was brought home by Danzas in almost a state of coma.

The news spread like wild fire. Pushkin's friends flocked to his home to learn that there was no hope. The poet suffered horribly, but with undiminished courage, and complete consciousness of impending death.

The Tsar sent him a short note advising him if the end came to try to die a Christian—advice which Pushkin followed. He died at 2:45 in the afternoon of January 29, 1837, conscious to the end.

Public indignation at his death reached fever pitch. Accusations were levelled against the government of failing, knowingly, to prevent the duel. Society turned on d'Anthès and de Heeckeren. d'Anthès was arrested, tried, found guilty, reduced to the ranks, and banished from Russia.

Pushkin's funeral, for fear of hostile demonstrations against the government, was kept a complete secret, his family and Turgenev being permitted to attend the last rites. The body was interred at Sviatogorsky Monastery near his beloved Mikhailovskoe.

A BIOGRAPHICAL SKETCH 57

The Tsar kept his word to the poet to look after his family; all his debts were paid, a pension granted to his widow and daughter, and his sons educated by the State. The poet's works were published for the benefit of the family, with a lump sum of 10,000 rubles paid in advance.

On the day of his funeral, a poem violently accusing the government of responsibility for the death of Russia's greatest genius was published. It was written by a young Lieutenant of the Guard Hussars, Lermontov, destined to be Pushkin's successor in greatness.

So passed Russia's first and greatest man of letters, and principal founder of the Russian literary language.

V

SPEECH DELIVERED JUNE 8, 1880 BEFORE THE SOCIETY OF LOVERS OF RUSSIAN LITERATURE AT MOSCOW BY FYODOR DOSTOYEVSKY*

PUSHKIN is an extraordinary, perhaps unique manifestation of the Russian spirit, said Gogol. I will add "and a prophetic manifestation." There is in his life, for all us Russians, something incontestibly prophetic. Pushkin appeared simultaneously with our achievement of self-consciousness, just a century after Peter's reforms, and helped us mightily in our darkness with his guiding light. Thus Pushkin has been to us a prophecy and a revelation.

I separate the activity of our great poet into three periods. I do not speak as a literary critic. I emphasize Pushkin's creative activity only to clarify my conception of his prophetic significance to us, and the interpretation I give to the word prophetic. I must, however, make the comment that

---

* In preparing this free rendering of Dostoyevsky's magnificent speech, the writer has thankfully availed himself of the assistance and inspiration afforded by numerous earlier translators. In especial, he is glad to admit his frequent obligation to the translations of Frances Henry Pritchard, (Great Essays of All Nations), and the joint labors of Messrs. S. Koteliansky and John Middleton Murry (Pages from the Journal of an Artist).

the periods of Pushkin's activity seem not to be differentiated with definiteness. The commencement of Eugene Onegin, for example, belongs to my mind to the first period, while its end should be placed in the second period, when Pushkin had discovered his ideals in his country, had absorbed them in his heart, and domiciled them in his affectionate and clear seeing soul. It may be that in his first period Pushkin was influenced by European poets, Parny and André Chénier, and by Byron above all. Doubtless these European poets greatly influenced his developing genius, and maintained that influence throughout his life. Not even Pushkin's very earliest poems were, however, mere imitations, and even in these the extraordinary originality of his genius expressed itself. Such personal suffering and such deep self-consciousness as Pushkin's are never found in an imitation; certainly not for instance in The Gypsies, a poem to be ascribed entirely to his first period, nor would his work have shown such force and impetuosity, had it been merely imitative. The character of Aleko, hero of The Gypsies, displays a strong, deep, and solely Russian concept, to appear later in harmonious perfection in Onegin, where nearly the same Aleko appears, not fantastically, but as definite, real and understandable. Pushkin had already realized with genius in Aleko the unhappy wanderer in the land of his nativity, the Russian sufferer of all time, whose re-incarnation, uprooted from the people's ranks, was a historic necessity. The character is true and admirably realized, it is an eternal character, long since native to Russia. These wanderers are wandering still, and it will be long before they disappear. In our day they no longer visit gypsy camps, seeking to discover their universal ideals and their consolation in that wild life, far from the confused and pointless activity of Russian intellectuals; now, with a new faith, they adopt socialism which did not exist in Aleko's day, and labor eagerly, thinking like Aleko that they may reach so their final goal, not for themselves alone, but for all men. Only so, in the happiness of all men can the Russian wanderer find peace; in theory at least he will be content with nothing less. It is the same essential man, appearing at a different time. This man was born at the beginning of the second century after Czar Peter's reforms, cast up from the people into a society of intellect. The greatest number of intellectual Russians in the time of Pushkin served then, just as now, as civil servants in government positions, in railways, banks, or other ways, or even engaged in science or lecturing —earning money in a regular peaceful leisured fashion, even playing cards, without desire for escape, whether to the gypsies or other refuge of more modern days. They only played at liberalism, "with a tinge of European socialism," which in Russia assumes a certain benignity—but that is after all only a matter of time. One man is not even yet annoyed while another, encountering a bolted door, furiously beats his head against it. All men meet destiny in their turn, unless they choose the saving road of humble identification with the people. Even though some escape, this must remain truth for the majority.

Aleko still fails completely to express his sorrow—he fails to achieve the concrete; he yearns for nature, cherishes a grudge against the higher classes, feels aspirations for all mankind; yearns too for the truth, somehow and somewhere lost, which he can nowhere find. He cannot tell wherein this truth resides, when this truth was lost, nor where she can be found, suffering nonetheless. Meanwhile a restless and fantastic creature searches for salvation in external things, as needs he must. Truth continues external to him, perhaps in some European country, with its more stable organization and settled mode of life. Nor can he understand that truth is after all within him. How could be understand this? For a century he has not been himself in his own country. He has no culture of his own. He has forgotten how to work. He has grown up within closed walls, as in a convent. He has had to fulfill unaccountable obligations, associated with one or another of the fourteen classes in educated Russian society. He is for the moment but a blade of grass torn from its roots, and blown upon the wind. He feels it, suffers for it, suffers acutely! What if for once he allowed himself the liberty of a nobleman, his privilege from birth, the pleasing whim of joining men who live "without laws," and leading a performing bear among the gypsies? A woman, "a wild woman" might bring him hope of deliverance from anguish, therefore he throws himself with fatalistic, passionate credulity into the arms of Zemphira. "Here is escape, here is happiness, here in the bosom of nature far from the crowd, here among men without law or civilization." What follows? He cannot bear the wild life of nature, and his hands are blood stained. The poor dreamer unequal to the "harmony of the spheres," is no more equal to the conditions of gypsydom; they cast him forth without malice, without desire for revenge, in simple dignity.

> "Depart, proud soul,
> We are lawless and wild,
> We torment you not nor punish."

Fantastic or not, the proud soul is genuine enough, his profile clearly limned. Let us remember that Poushkin was the first to immortalize this type. The man is ready to torture and punish others for his wrongs, whene'er he is displeased, for he can never forget his membership in the fourteen classes, and will himself appeal to law—it has happened often—to revenge his private wrong with its punishment and torture. No, this is genius in verse,—no imitation! Here indeed we have the answer to the Russian question, "the accursed question," in terms of the faith and the equity of the people. "Humble yourself, proud soul, humble your pride. Humble yourself in your idleness, and labor on your native land"—that is the answer of the people, in justice and in wisdom. "Truth is within thee, not without. Find thyself in thyself. Humble thyself to thyself. Be master of thine own soul, and see the truth. Not without, nor abroad is this truth, not in things, but in thee and in thine own labor upon thyself. If thou conquerest thyself, then wilt thou be free beyond dreams, and make others free; thou wilt labor upon a great task, and will find in it happiness and fulfillment, and, at long last, understanding of thine own people and their holy truth. If thou art thyself unworthy, proud, and given to malice, if thou demandest life as a gift, without payment, neither with the gypsies nor in any other place whatsoever shalt thou discover the 'harmony of the spheres'." This answer is clearly seen in Pushkin's poem. It is seen yet more clearly in Eugene Onegin, a realistic and tangible tale, in no sense a fantasy, in which the life of Russia is recreated with a force and a truth beyond any predecessor and perhaps equally beyond any successor to Pushkin.

Onegin is of Petersburg—inevitably of Petersburg: It is imperative for the poem that its hero so derives, nor could Pushkin avoid it. Onegin is, I repeat, the same Aleko, most especially where he cries out in anguish:

> "Why am I not, like the assessor of Tula,
> Stricken with palsy?"

Only at the poem's beginning is he still a man of the world, and half a coxcomb; as yet he has not lived long enough for complete disillusion, but he already knows

> "The Satanic king of secret weariness . . ."

In the remote heart of his fatherland, he is yet in exile. Conscious of his aim, he yet knows not where to turn. Later, he still feels himself in the midst of strangers, even more a stranger to himself, despite his brains and his sincerity, wherever he may roam, at home or abroad. He loves his country, but cannot trust it. He knows its ideals, but he has no faith in them. He cannot see the possibility of any work in his own country, and he can feel only sorrow and derision for those few who can believe in it. Lensky he had killed out of spleen born of yearning for the unattainable—that was very Russian, altogether probable.

Tatiana is quite another person—strong of character, strongly bestriding her own ground. Deeper than Onegin, and wiser, she divines truth with a noble instinct, and her mind finds full expression in the poem's end. Perhaps that poem might better have been called Tatiana, not Onegin,—she is so undeniably the protagonist. Positive, not negative, the beautiful apotheosis of Russian womanhood, the poet's conception of her and of his poem is expressed in the superb scene of her final meeting with Onegin. So beautiful, so finished a type of Russian womanhood does not appear in all our literature, except perhaps for Liza in Turgeniev's "A Nest of Gentle Folk." Onegin never understood Tatiana, since he looked down on her from above—not even when he met her first, a pure, shy, innocent girl in a remote place. He could not realize her complete perfection—perhaps he even took her for a "moral embryo." She, the embryo! She, after her letter to Onegin! It is Onegin who is the embryo, if there be one, Onegin beyond all doubt. And he could not understand her. Does he know the soul? All his life he has been a restless dreamer, living in abstractions. No more can he understand her later as a grand lady in Petersburg, despite the words of his letter to her "he and his soul understood all her perfections." These are but words. Unrecognized by him and unappreciated, she crossed his stage—therein lay the tragedy of their love. Only if Childe Harold or, by some miracle, Lord Byron himself had pointed out to him at their first meeting, her timid modest beauty, would Onegin have been struck with admiration,—so much spiritual servility resides in these universal sufferers. Without this he could only have read her a sermon, after which the seeker for universal harmony, having done very honestly by her, departs with his anguish and with the blood of his friend, spilt in senseless anger, on his hands, to wander, forgetful of Tatiana far afield; and, full to the brim with health and strength, exclaims with a curse:

> "Young am I yet, and life is strong within me
> Yet anguish, anguish, anguish, still awaits me."

Tatiana understood. In the deathless verse of his romantic tale, she is shown coming to behold the house of the lover who is still to her so marvellous, and yet so ill to understand. The depth and beauty, the supreme art of the verse, needs not to be spoken of here. She is in his study; she sees his books and his possessions; she seeks still, through them, to pierce his soul, to answer her everlasting question, and "the moral embryo" gently whispers after a thoughtful pause, with a foreboding that it is at last her answer:

> "Perhaps he is only a parody?"

Yes, it was this that she whispered—she had understood him. When again, long afterwards in St. Petersburg they meet once more, she knows him completely. Who was it that said that life at court and in society, that her new position as a lady of fashion, had so changed her soul, that the new ideas so engendered were partly the reason for her refusal of Onegin? It is not true. She is the same Tanya, the same country Tanya as before! She is not spoiled; no, she is tortured by the magnificent life of St. Petersburg, she is tormented by it, and she suffers; she hates her position in society, and no one who understands what Pushkin was trying to say, could think otherwise. With firmness, she tells Onegin:

> "Now am I to another given:
> To him I will be faithful unto death."

This is indeed the sum total of her character, in the typical phrase of a Russian woman. Her character symbolizes the truth of the verses. I shall not touch upon her religious convictions, her feeling about the sacrament of marriage. After she herself had said to him "I love you," did she nevertheless refuse to follow him? Was it because, "as a Russian woman" she was incapable of so bold a step, or lacked force to sacrifice the allure of honor, riches, social position, the convention of virtue? No, she was brave like all Russian women; she would boldly do what she believed, and her actions prove it. Rather she "is to another given; to him she will be faithful unto death." To what, to whom, will she be true? To what code be faithful? Is her obligation to that elderly general, whom she could not possibly love, whom she had married because "with tears and abjurations her mother did beseech her," and in her wounded and betrayed soul was there only despair, without hope or a ray of light? She is indeed true to the general, her husband, in the character of an honest man who loves and respects her, and has pride in her. Her mother "did beseech her" indeed, but it was she alone who consented with an oath to be his faithful wife. Though she had married him in despair, he is her husband, and the shame and disgrace of any perfidy on her part would be his death. Can any happiness be truly built on the unhappiness of another? Happiness lies rather in the higher harmony of the spirit than in the delights of love. How could that spirit be content after an inhuman, merciless, dishonorable act? Dare one run away for happiness alone? What kind of happiness would that be? Conceive that you will build a monument to destiny with the end of giving all men happiness, rest and peace. Conceive again that it is necessary and inevitable thereby to torture one single being, not great and even perhaps ridiculous, no Shakespeare but simply the honest, old husband of a young wife whom he trusts implicitly, and whom, knowing her heart not at all, he yet respects, is proud and happy and at peace in her company. He has to be dishonored, disgraced, and tortured, that upon his suffering your palace may be built. Would you be satisfied to be the architect of that palace on such conditions? That is the final question. If that palace were built upon suffering, though but the suffering of an insignificant person, cruelly and unjustly put to death, could you for an instant believe that the inhabitants of the building would thank you for happiness on such terms? Could the great heart of Tatiana so enobled by suffering, have answered otherwise? No, the soul of the pure Russian woman replies: "I will not be happy through having ruined an old man; though he know not nor appreciate my sacrifice, let me alone be deprived of happiness, rather than that he suffer." So the tragedy transpires—Tatiana sends Onegin away. One may say she has saved one at the expense of another—Onegin, too, is unhappy. That involves the most important question, perhaps, in the whole poem. That question, why did not Tatiana run away with Onegin, has, in our literature, a most characteristic importance, wherefor I allow myself to consider it at length. The most important fact is that the answer to that question should so long have been doubtful. To my mind, even had Tatiana been released by her husband's death, even then she would not have gone away with Onegin. It was in her character to realize Onegin as he was. He, the eternal wanderer, had discerned in a new and more precious setting, the jewel he had scorned. That setting was perhaps the essence: the present jewel, socially adored, is the same he had despised, but now sanctioned by the halo of society, the final authority for him of all his aspirations. Therefore, dazzled, he is at her feet. Here at last, he cries, is my ideal, my future, my escape from everlasting agony. Formerly, when "happiness was so possible, so near," I failed to see her truly. Thus Onegin turns now to Tatiana, as Aleko turned to Zemphira, hoping to find in this new fancy the answer to his destiny. Does Tatiana realize this, has she not realized it long since? Beyond a doubt she realizes that it is not her he loves, but her new incarnation. She sees that he loves no one, is incapable of loving anyone, despite his suffering, that it is not she whom he loves, but her position. It is a fancy, as he himself is but a fancy, that he loves. Were she to go away with him, tomorrow he would be disillusioned, and mock at his own infatuation. He is but a blade of grass, without roots, blown upon the wind. Even in her despair in the wounded contemplation of a ruined life, she is herself, solid, unshakeable. Even in her childhood was she thus, even in her memories of her remote natal village, that village in which her pure and simple life began: it is

> "The woven shade of branches that o'erhang her nurse's grave."

Priceless to her now are these memories and pictures of the past—nought else is left to save her from despair. That is her single foundation, permanent and unshakeable. Therein is her contact with her birthplace, her family, the ideals of her youth. And what by contrast has he to offer? Nothing save that she may follow him out of her pity, and use him, gratify him with an illusive happiness out of her pitying love, with fore-knowledge that tomorrow he himself will deride his illusive happiness. No, her deep true soul could never sanction dishonor, even in the infinity of compassion. No, Tatiana could never go away with Onegin.

Thus in this incomparable, this immortal poem, did Pushkin reveal himself as an unexcelled, supreme, and truly national writer. With exactness and insight, he etched, in this tour de force, the very inmost essence of Russian society. Imperishably he delineated the Russian wanderer of all time; with the flair of genius, he realized the type, and its tremendous significance in the national destiny. Alongside that type, he posed the rare beauty of Russian womanhood. As in his other works, he set down a very gallery of exquisite types drawn from the Russian people. The exquisiteness is in their truth, their positive and undeniable truth. You cannot deny them, they stand as though in stone. I feel no duty upon me to clarify my thought by a detailed and critical dissertation on these works of Pushkin's genius. As well might one write an entire book in the spirit of the old monkish chroniclers, to establish the meaning of one of the noble figures unearthed by Pushkin, and established for all time in exquisite beauty, as evidence of that most potent spirit of Russia which can project types of just such indubitable beauty. Such a type is herein set forth, exists for all time beyond cavil, in reality not in fancy. In that existence lives and flourishes the spirit of his nation vast, potent, and eternal. All the writing of Pushkin affirms the spiritual force of Russia and the Russian character; that character expressed in the eternal lines:

> "In the hope of glory and good
> I look ahead without fear."

No Russian writer was ever so intimately at one with the Russian people as Pushkin. Those multitudinous writers who have taken the people as their theme, compared with Pushkin, are, with one or at most two exceptions, only "gentlemen" writing about the masses. Even in the two gifted exceptions * I have just mentioned, there is apt to appear on occasion a flash of haughtiness, which seems like an effort to bring happiness to the people by raising them to the writer's level. But in Pushkin there resides an emotionalism almost naif, which makes him seem the ally and equal of the people. Remember his story of "The Bear" and the killing of the bear's mate by a peasant; or recall the line,

> "Kinsman John, when we begin to drink . . ."

and you will comprehend my meaning.

All these gems of art and insight remain as a

---

* Turgeniev and Tolstoi are meant.

land mark for Pushkin's successors, for the writers of later days. It is not too much to say that without Pushkin the gifted authors who succeeded him would never have transpired. At best, despite all their gifts of expression, they would have lacked the power and clarity from him derived. Without him we should have lost not literature alone, but much of our irresistible force, our faith in our national individuality, our belief in the people's powers, and most of all our belief in our destiny. All this is most especially true of the great achievement of what I have called the third period of Pushkin's activity.

As I have said, there are no positive divisions between the periods. Pushkin was always a complete whole, homogeneous, individual—so that some of the works of even his last period are almost indistinguishable from those of his first. Impulses from without called forth in him only the response of what was already within him. His development, in all its phases, could be recognized best by its indigenous peculiarities, and the normal development of each period out of its predecessor. Thus his third period reflects chiefly universal ideas, in which the genius of other nations is re-embodied and reflected. Some of the works of this period appeared only after the poet's death. And in this period, Pushkin revealed a miracle, a capacity for universal sympathy unequalled even by the colossi of Europe—Schiller, Cervantes, Shakespeare. By this capacity, pre-eminently Russian, he marks himself our true national poet. No poet of Europe could, equally with Pushkin, embody in himself the genius and the hidden spirit of neighboring peoples. European poets, on the contrary, were at one with their own people and with no one else. Even in the case of Shakespeare, his Italians remain almost always Englishmen. The characters of Pushkin alone possess the individuality of their nations. Read again his "Don Juan," his "Miser Knight," his ballad "Once There Lived a Poor Knight," his scenes from Faust. Without Pushkin's signature, you might have supposed them written by a Spaniard. How deep and strange is his fantasy in the poem "A Feast in Time of Plague." But in this fantasy you discover the genius of England; as in the hero's marvellous song of the plague, and in Mary's song,

"Our children's voices in the noisy school
    Were heard. . . ."

These songs are English; they express the longing of British genius, its tears, its unhappy forecast of its future. Recall the symbolical lines:

"Once I wandered through the valley wild."

These verses, with their sad, ecstatic music are the key to the first pages of a mystical book, written in prose by an old Englishman and sectarian. These lines aren't solely a key, for they embody the very soul of Northern Protestantism, of British doctrinal controversy, and the slow-witted, dour mystic, with his spiritual dreams and their impulsive power, and his determined but unbounded aspirations. You hear in the sound of these verses the very spirit of the times, of the Reformation.— They bring home the hostile fury of early Protestantism, and you understand why Thought was swept by the times, walked through their sectarian camps, sang their Psalms, wept with them in their religious ecstasies, and joined in their belief. Compare this religious mysticism with the religious verses from the Koran or "Imitations from the Koran," and do we not find a similarity to Mohammedanism in the very spirit of its naïve grandeur of faith and its appalling power? We find also, the ancient world; the Egyptian Nights, where the gods of earth sit, who ruled over their people like gods, despising their aspirations and their genius. These gods, in isolation, exerted their power, until they were overcome by madness from their utter weariness of isolation, and strove to drive it off by diverting themselves with inordinate brutalities, the sensual fascination of creeping things, of a female spider devouring its male. Emphatically I say, there never has been a poet like Poushkin, with his universal sympathy, his extraordinary profundity, and the miraculous reincarnation of his spirit in the spirit of other nations —miraculous, because the gift has never been repeated in any other poet in the world. This universality is only in Poushkin; therefore I repeat, he is a phenomenon, a prophetic phenomenon, because he expressed in his poetry the National spirit—the National spirit in its future development, and the National spirit of our future, which, already, has come to pass. For there is no power in the spirit of Russian nationality, if not to aspire to universality, and an all embracing humanitarianism. No sooner had Poushkin become a really National poet, than he discovered the National power, and in anticipating the great future of that power, he was a true prophet, a real diviner.

Let us look at the vast reform of Peter the Great, not only for its effect on the future, but on that which has already been plainly shown to us. What did this great reform mean to us? Surely not just the adoption of European inventions, science, and ways of life. Let us examine it closely, it may be probable that Peter began his reform in this restricted, every-day sense, but with time, his idea grew, and, with it, his inner instinct was drawing him and his task to future purposes, with grander and broader perceptions. Thus the Russian people did not confine their acceptance of the reform to its first and narrower conception; but, with an instinctive presentiment, they felt forewarned of a distant, but incomparably higher goal than that of every-day habit and custom. Although unconscious, the purpose was implicit and vital. We then began

SPEECH DELIVERED 1880

surely and vigorously to turn to the unity of all Mankind. Not in a hostile spirit, but in a spirit of friendliness and perfect love. We absorbed in our very being, the geniuses of foreign nations without preference of race. In our eagerness to unite with the great Aryan family, we were quickly able by instinct to discern, to discount distinctions, and to excuse and reconcile them. Beyond all doubt, the destiny of a Russian is pan-European and universal. To become a true Russian, is to become the brother of all men, a universal man. All our narrower nationalism, as our Slavophilism, though necessary to history, is only a great misunderstanding. For Europe and the destiny of all the powerful Aryan family is as close to the hearts of all true Russians as the future of Russia herself. Our future lies in Universality, not won by violence, but by the strength derived from our great ideal—the re-uniting of all mankind.

If you delve into our history, since Peter's reforms, you will find this ideal, this dream of mine already beginning to make itself felt—both by the nature of our relations with Europe, and by the policies of state. For Russian policy for the last two centuries has been one of service to Europe, perhaps exceeding any service she has given herself. I do not believe that this was a result of the incapacity of our statesmen, but rather that the nations of Europe know how to value them. And given time, I feel sure that our future generations will all realize and understand that to be a true Russian, means the hope of achieving the reconciliation of the contradictions of Europe, and putting an end to the hankering for Europe, which lingers in our souls, and to take unto ourselves, in a spirit of brotherly love and harmony, all our brethren, and unite in a spirit of International peace and communion, in accordance with the law of the gospel of Christ. My goal may seem too ecstatic, too incredible and too elusive, but let it appear so. I have no apologies to make. The goal must be reiterated time and again, especially now, the moment we have chosen to honour Poushkin, whose genius and artistic powers, were the embodiment of this ideal. The idea is not new, it has been given expression many times in the past. My fear is that lack of originality may appear presumptuous. "Is this our destiny, the destiny of our poor land? Are we predestined among mankind to utter the new world?"

I speak only of the brotherhood of man, not of the triumphs of the sword, the achievements of science, or of economic grandeurs. For I am convinced that the heart of Russia, more than any other nation, is dedicated to this universal union of all mankind; I see this from our history, our great men, and the artistic spirit of Poushkin. Our land may not flourish, but this poor land "Christ traversed with blessing, in the garb of a serf." Should we then, not content ourselves with His word? Was not He Himself born in a manger? I repeat, at least we have Poushkin, his philosophy, and genius of universality, and all-embracing humanitarianism to point to. He harboured in his soul, as his own, the genius of many lands, revealing in his creative efforts the universality of the aspiration of the Russian spirit. We may well take joy in this, as a promise for the future. If our goal appears a dream, Poushkin at least lends it reality. If he had lived longer, he might, through the power of his genius, have been able to immortalize the spirit of the Russian soul, bringing it closer and making it more comprehensible to our European family; perhaps succeeding in attracting them to us, more than they are now, and enabling them to see the truth of our hopes and desires—even giving them a better insight into our natures, that they might learn to regard us with less suspicion and with better understanding. Had Poushkin lived longer, or had we been able to fathom his great secret, we might find that among Russians too, there would be less strife and less misunderstanding. But God willed it otherwise, and Poushkin, at the heighth of his career, died—and his great secret was lost to posterity.

VI

PUSHKIN AND RUSSIAN MUSIC
By Olin Downes

THE revival of "Coq d'Or" this week at the Metropolitan is one of the musical events which signalize in this country the hundredth anniversary of the death of the mighty Puskin. His fantastical and satirical poem is the subject matter of Rimsky-Korsakoff's last opera.

There is a singular analogy between the position of one of the greatest of poets when he produced this work and that of the composer who set it. Both men, in their respective situations, and nearing the end of life, were beset by official restraints and suppressions which inhibited creative expression. They were weary and saddened by the shams and obstructions of Lilliputians who surrounded them, which gradually sapped vitality and inspiration.

It is known that the government's interference with the production of his opera irritated Rimsky-Korsakoff and hastened his end. It is perhaps a providential if extremely tragic circumstance that the poet who is root and branch of all Russian literature and music, too, should have received the wound from which he died, while still young, in the duel with d'Anthès, 100 years ago last Wednesday.

An invisible net had been spread about the poet who was born to be free. This was seen to by Nicholas I and his court—the net of apparent tolerance, of luxury, security and social privilege while the Decembrists perished or went to Siberia. The system of the iron hand beneath the courtly glove was applied to the pardoned Pushkin. The obstacles, politely veneered, which confronted him wherever he turned, would have frustrated, softened and eventually ruined him. The supremely creative spirit could go no farther. It was as if fate had determined to intervene and prevent a worse than physical disintegration. A bitter commentary which doubtless emanated from circumstances that inspired revolt, colors the poem of "Coq d'Or," which was censored. Similar circumstances, following Russia's abortive revolution of 1905-1906, had to do with the early history of the opera.

. . . . .

But, then, you can no more separate Russian music from Pushkin than you can a tree from its roots. Never was there a more incontrovertible demonstration of the common sources of poetry and music. Never was an art more conclusively demonstrative of the connection between the artist and his expression and his soil. No Russian literature of importance since Pushkin is explicable without him, and he is so interwoven with the development of Russian music that the one can hardly be referred to without thought of the constant presence and the inexhaustible potency of the other.

> "Near a sea-cove an oak is growing;
> Around that oak a golden chain:
> Along that chain Sir-Cat-the-Knowing
> Doth ever walk and walk again.
> Goes to the right—a song he chaunteth,
> Goes to the left a tale he tells. . . .
> There I have been; there I drank mead,
> Saw the green oak near sea-cove growing,
> And sat beneath; Sir-Cat-the-Knowing
> Did with his wondrous tales proceed."

The famous prologue to "Russlan and Ludmilla," affixed to the second edition of the poem which stirred all literary Russia and divided it immediately into two camps, furnished music that was equally historic. Glinka, younger than Pushkin, knew and associated with him (1823) in Petersburg. The day was yet to come when Glinka would awaken from the thralldom of Italian opera and other foreign cultural currents and do for music what Pushkin was already doing in his poetry, but that time was not far off. In 1836 came the opera "The Life for the Czar," which is the cornerstone of Russian national opera and the true beginning of the Russian school of composition. Its plot was based upon the the poem of Pushkin's associate, the older Zhukovsky. Then, in 1842, appeared the opera in which Glinka wholly identified himself with the new movement and in which are found the germs of so much of the later music of the nineteenth-century school—"Russlan and Ludmilla." Thereafter every prominent composer and song writer of the century was to dip deep and always deeper for inspiration in the spring of Pushkin's genius.

. . . . .

Primarily for the reason of inadequate and until now incomplete translation, there is the general impression in English-speaking countries that Pushkin's eminence is principally that of a national bard. This, of course, is anything but the case. Pushkin had indeed listened to tales of the fabulous cat. He had heard them from his nurse, Arina Rodionovna, in his childhood. She, indeed, was his friend and comforter as long as she lived, and she joined him in the enforced sojourn in the Caucasus. Besides this, the folklore of Oriental as of Occidental Russia was Pushkin's constant interest.

It was profoundly associated with the nature from which it came, mirrored in the marvelous Caucasian land, experienced in Bessarabia in his actual wanderings with a gypsy tribe which gave rise to a famous poem, and in a thousand other experiences of a life lived with singular intensity. But Pushkin, descendant on the one side of six hundred years of noble ancestors, and on the other of Abraham Gannibil, the Abyssinian—"Peter the Great's nigger" (actually the son of an Ethiopian King captured by the Turks and sold as a slave) —was brilliantly educated, precocious in letters. The early literary influences were Parny, André Chénier, Voltaire, whom he fanatically admired. During the first Caucasian visit he learned English, and was imbued with Byronism. In due course he relinquished Byron for Shakespeare, whose influence is manifest in "Boris Godunoff." Dante and Goethe were familiars.

. . . . .

It may be said that what these men did for his natural literature Pushkin did for Russia and the Russian tongue, first revealed by him in all its naturalness, variety and beauty. He fused the idioms of popular and cultivated art in one manifectation, and this as early as "Russlan," a product of his youthful years and of European as well as native influences.

He was a magnificently schooled technician, a virtuoso in his craft, but never a sophisticate, never less than an adorer of life and a Russian prophet of mankind. No wonder that when he read the first version of "Russlan" to the older Zhukovsky, the latter inscribed his portrait, "To a victorious pupil from a defeated master."

Pushkin's universality is rooted in the earth, is Russian in a way and to a degree that the intensive, highly developed but more exclusive culture of Europe does not know. His humanity and vivid perception of nature, his adoration of life as supreme teacher, underlay the simplicity, vigor and raciness of his style. They present him in powerful contrast to a European culture which, for lack of fresh currents, is drying up at the roots. Not the least impressive proof of his significance lies in the utter change of the present Russian Government toward him since the earlier days of the revolution. Then Pushkin was virtually banned. Now he is exalted, as also the sources of racial strength which inspired him—the folklore, customs, melodies of his country.

. . . . .

Were there time and space, Pushkin's universality of mind, and the mingling of racial understanding and intuitive and objective contemplation of mankind could be better defined through allusions to the nature of various poems. So that, from revolutionary fanaticism, as well as the preoccupations and the somewhat supercilious attitude, in the past, of European culture toward the Russian, Pushkin rises always higher and more secure in the regard of his country and the world.

Has any other poet been identified more completely with the music of his native land? It is nevertheless probable that Pushkin's sun is rising rather than setting. It is the fact that among musicians only Mussorgsky, in "Boris Godunoff," and Tchaikovsky, with less dramatic success, have come near the true inwardness of the greater aspects of Pushkin. But he has inspired generations.

Mention of a few compositions inspired by his masterpieces is scarcely an indication of the extent to which his influence has been felt. But consider certain of the more prominent instances.

Glinka sets "Russlan" as the most appropriate possible theme for a leader of the Russian school of opera. Dargomijsky sets "The Stone Guest," in its exact original text—the story of Don Juan—and also "Russalka." Tchaikovsky takes "Eugen Onégin," "Pique Dame" and "Mazeppa," from the poem "Poltava." Cui sets "The Captain's Daughter" and "The Prisoner of the Caucasus." Rimsky-Korsakoff uses "Tsar Saltan," "Mozart and Salieri," "Coq d'Or," captions his orchestral "Skazka" with the "Russlan" prologue, and sets many of the poems as songs.

Mussorgsky uses many poems for songs and creates from the text and subject of "Boris Godunoff" his operatic masterpiece. Rachmaninoff's operas "Aleko" and "The Miser Knight" are after Pushkin. Stravinsky sets "Faun and Shepherdess" for voices and instruments, and makes a one-act opera of "Mavra."

It would be easier, in fact, to mention Russian song composers who have not used Pushkin texts, than to enumerate those, great and small, who have. This refers even to the moderns—the Dukelskys, Gniessins, etc.—as it does to the older men, present and past, the Rachmaninoffs, Gretchaninoffs, Medtners, Tcherepnines, Glazunoffs and Arenskys.

And why? Because of his ancestral power, the greatness of his soul, the genuineness and vitality of his wingéd words and their music. Because of his perception of wonder in the innermost things, his capacity to perceive in a flash the eternal significance of a gesture or everyday occurrence; because he was a master poet and universal spokesman for humanity in terms of his race. His words live and immortally sing.

· · · · ·

"This capacity," said Dostoievsky, in his memorable speech at the Pushkin ceremonies of 1880, "the pre-eminent capacity of our nation, he shares with our nation, and by that above all he is our national poet * * * For what is the power of the spirit of Russian nationality if not its aspiration after the goal of * * * omni-humanity?"

When Pushkin died there was fear of a popular demonstration, so that his remains were carefully removed to the cemetery in the night-time. Two words, "To Pushkin," sufficed the many who hurried on the night of his death to watch before his house, to shout to the overworked cabmen.

Perhaps Russian music will again realize its soul, lost in political and other confusions, when it returns to the spirit reflected in the manifold aspects of the great poet's genius. Then again, as now, it will be time to say, in salutation and gratitude, "To Pushkin."

VII

THE STONE GUEST OF PUSHKIN
By Edith Fahnestock, Ph.D.
Professor of Spanish, Vassar College

THIS short dramatic sketch of Pushkin's written in 1830 and published posthumously is interesting in itself and also in its relation to the other forms which the story of Don Juan has taken on in many of the literatures of Europe.

Pushkin's version is an extremely concentrated one:

> "Don Juan and his servant Leporello are in a convent cemetery at the gates of Madrid waiting for the cover of night in order to enter the city from which he has been banned by the king. Leporello timidly dwells on the consequences to Don Juan if caught. The latter answers lightly at first and then romantically recalls Ines, now dead, whom he had loved. Leporello interjects: 'There were others before her and there will be still others.' He asks what beauty they are to visit in Madrid and learns that they are going to Laura. A monk approaches them and asks if they belong to Donna Anna's attendants. He adds that Donna Anna (whose husband had been slain by that God-forsaken Don Juan) comes daily to pray at the tomb which she has erected to his

memory. When Don Juan wishes to speak with Donna Anna, the monk assures him that it is impossible. Donna Anna has nothing to do with men. Don Juan's desire shocks even Leporello. At dusk they enter Madrid. Leporello in an aside says: 'That a Spanish grandee should wait for the shades of night and fear the moon like a common thief!'

"The second scene shows Laura after the theatre entertaining a group of friends and her lover Don Carlos. She sings a song which she says Don Juan composed. Carlos hates Don Juan as the former lover of Laura and the slayer of his brother in a duel. But Laura appeases him and, left alone, they open the balcony windows to enjoy the loveliness of the night. At this moment Don Juan from below demands admittance. Laura falls on Don Juan's neck. Carlos challenges him to a duel and is killed.

"In the third scene Don Juan, disguised as a monk, again takes refuge in the convent cemetery. After watching every day as she prays before the statue of her husband, he decides to speak to her. She asks him to join her in her prayers, but he replies that his lips are too sinful. From his next words she guesses that he is no monk and he kneels to ask her forgiveness, saying that he is a poor wretched creature, the victim of a hopeless passion. She begs him to go. He pleads that only now does he understand the worth of this fleeting life—only now does he know happiness. Touched by his love she promises to talk with him again the next night at her house. He gives his name as Diego Calvado. Don Juan in a burst of exaltation tells Leporello of his happiness. The

THE STONE GUEST

servant ironically remarks that widows are all alike and asks what the Commander (the statue of the husband) will have to say. The Commander assumes a threatening attitude. Don Juan jauntily orders Leporello to invite him to come to keep watch at Donna Anna's door. Leporello in spite of his fear, gives the invitation. The statue's nod paralyzes Leporello with fear. Don Juan refuses to believe his eyes and gives the invitation himself. The statue nods again.

"In the last scene Donna Anna dispels Don Juan's jealousy of her former husband by telling him that she had married at her mother's bidding because they were poor. Don Juan, now genuinely moved, confesses his sense of guilt. He explains that he is Don Juan, her only enemy. Notwithstanding his admission she shows solicitude for his safety. She consents to see him again. Just as he kisses her there is an ominous knocking at the door. The statue of the Commander enters and says that he has come at Don Juan's invitation. Don Juan exclaims: 'God, Donna Anna!' The statue bids him leave Donna Anna's name out. All is over. He also accuses Don Juan of trembling. Don Juan denies this and asserts that he is glad to see his guest. The statue replies: 'Give me your hand.' Don Juan does so exclaiming: 'How heavy is the pressure of his cold and stony hand! . . . Let go my hand. . . . I'm perishing, dying, Donna Anna!' Don Juan and the statue sink into the ground."

Gendarme de Bévotte has made a careful study of the legend Don Juan and the literary forms in which the hero has appeared in most European countries. He says of Pushkin's *Stone Guest:*

"C'est un drame ramassé et puissant qui peut compter parmi les plus vigoureuses et les plus originales productions de son auteur. Par le lyrisme et la force de la passion, par le caractère du héros sincèrement épris de la femme qu'il désire, par les modifications apportés au sujet, l'oeuvre rompt avec la tradition." *

It may be of interest to determine, if possible, which are the elements of the story that Pushkin owes to the tradition before him and which versions had most influence upon him.

The first question that arises is whether Pushkin knew the original Spanish drama in which Tirso de Molina created the hero who, with astonishing vigor, still appeals to the most varied kinds of writers. Tirso's *Burlador de Sevilla y el convidado de piedra (Don Juan and the Stone Guest)* was probably written before 1630, the date of its oldest known edition. Tirso was a highly respected monk who as a dramatist of the Golden Age of Spanish literature ranks next to Lope de Vega and Calderón. His version of the Don Juan legend is the most complete of all and it is he who combined with this legend a second, *The Stone Guest.*

"The first two acts of the *Burlador* are thoroughly in the style of the ordinary cloak and

* Gendarme de Bévotte, La légende de Don Juan, Paris, 1911, vol. 2, p. 14.

THE STONE GUEST

sword drama of his time and treat of the adventures in which Don Juan betrayed successively the Italian Duchess Isabella, the fisher maiden Tisbea, the humble bride Aminta, and attempted to deceive Donna Anna, but was prevented by her father the Comendador Gonzalo, whom he killed. Juan is always valiant, exuberant, proud of his name and his exploits, insatiable in his zest for new experiences in love, light and frivolous at times, at other times almost a Titan in strength. But in the last act, the greater part of which is given to the *Stone Guest* legend, we have a kind of morality play, or rather a short *auto* of solemn religious tone (in spite of comic elements) which is thoroughly Spanish. The only preparation for this conclusion which appears in the first acts is the hint of impending doom and punishment given constantly by Don Juan's companion, his servant Catalinón in his warnings and admonitions. Don Juan, who is no atheist or unbeliever does not question the idea of divine wrath and chastisement, but meets Catalinón each time with: 'But that's a long time off.'

"When Don Juan and Catalinón return to Seville after their necessary absence following the death of the Comendador, they see the statue erected by the king in his honor in a chapel which they happen to pass. They read the inscription: 'Here lies a most loyal gentleman waiting for the Lord to take vengeance on a traitor.' Don Juan jests and mockingly calls out an invitation to the statue to sup with him that night at his inn. Then follow comic scenes showing the fright of the servants when, as supper is served in the inn, an ominous knock at the door is heard. Catalinón is so terrified that he can not tell what he sees on opening the door. Don Juan takes the candle and goes himself. He starts back, puts his hand on the hilt of his sword, but quickly recovers himself when the statue announces that he is the invited guest. Don Juan tries to quiet his servants: 'Why fear a dead man?' The statue asks for a promise and Don Juan gives his word of honor that he will accept the invitation of the statue to sup with him on the next night in the chapel. Don Juan lights him to the door. Alone, however, he shivers: 'When he took my hand he pressed it so that it felt like hell itself . . . his breath was cold, etc.' But he concludes that all this must have been an hallucination and regains his courage. On the next evening he drags the unwilling Catalinón with him to the chapel. The Comendador commands Don Juan to lift the top of the tomb, and as he does so his host admits that he is really brave. The gruesome meal consists of scorpions and vipers, the drink of gall and vinegar, the songs that accompany the feast are dirges telling of the wrath of God and His punishments. Don Juan's courage endures, however, even when he has to clasp again that burning hand. He tells Gonzalo that he really had not betrayed his daughter, but Gonzalo says that it does not matter since it was his intention to do so. Don Juan ready to meet his doom asks to be confessed and to receive absolution but the Comendador replies that it is too late now. Don Juan calls out: 'I am consumed with fire' and falls dead. Catalinón escapes and later tells how the whole chapel ablaze sank into the ground with both the Comendador and Don Juan."

THE STONE GUEST 95

Like another of Tirso's dramas, the *Man condemned for lack of Faith,* the *Burlador* in its serious part is a weighing of that problem which so preoccupied the Spanish of his time—the part that faith and works have in the salvation of man. In the former drama the man who repents of his evil deeds is saved, whereas the holy man of good works is damned for his doubts. Here Don Juan is condemned for having too confidently put off repentance until the last moment.

Before going on with the question of Pushkin's acquaintance with Tirso, it is necessary to take up some of the modifications of the story made in Italy and France since some of these versions were known in Russia in Pushkin's time. In Italy where Tirso's drama passed almost immediately, it was known as "The Stone Guest" (Convitato di pietra). A drama by Cicognini has come down to us, and the description of a scenario. Another version of Giliberti has been lost. The greatest change which affected the drama was the loss of the solemnity and the religious element so important to Tirso's conception. Don Juan seems of less interest than his servant Passarino through whom the development of more comic scenes becomes possible. He is no longer the timid but loyal servant who follows his master almost like the voice of conscience at times. The cowardice is exaggerated, the comic elements developed and his fervent desire is to be rid of such a master. When Don Juan dies Passarino's only thought is for his wages.

In 1658 Italian actors of the Petit Bourbon theatre gave a *Convié de Pierre,* and in 1659 Villiers' *Festin de Pierre* was played in the Hotel de Bourgogne. Molière's *Festin de Pierre* followed in 1665. Two points in Pushkin's drama would seem to show acquaintance with Villiers. The name of the Comendador in both is Don Alvar, and Don Juan after he fled from the house of Laura, is disguised as a monk, a disguise which he also used in Villiers' version. It is well known that Pushkin was thoroughly familiar with Molière. With Molière the character of Don Juan, although more carefully developed, has changed greatly. He is still valiant and has become a more real person, but one more like a seventeenth century Frenchman. He is now frankly atheist, and at times hypocritical. Pushkin's Don Juan is different from Tirso's, but he does not resemble the Don Juan of these versions either. He is Pushkin's—both poetic and capable of a sincere love. Of the women who appear in these dramas only Donna Anna survives in Pushkin, and she is no longer the daughter of the fine old Comendador, but the widow of the rich Commandante whom Don Juan had killed in a duel. The development of Donna Anna's character is entirely Pushkin's. The servant Leporello remains true to tradition in character if not in name. Cowardly, free-spoken, with no

THE STONE GUEST

feeling of loyalty but rather with a desire to leave his master, he is still the critic of Don Juan's actions. The stone guest who played so large a part in the versions before Pushkin, comes in only at the last when he is invited by Don Juan not to sup but to stand guard the next night at Donna Anna's door when he visits her. There is the same ghostly knock at the door, the same burning clasp of the statue's hand, and the same disappearance of both Don Juan and the Commandante. Don Juan manifests the same valor to the end.

From internal evidence it would seem that nothing in Pushkin's drama points positively to a knowledge at first hand of Tirso's *Burlador*. It is known, however, that Pushkin learned Spanish in order to read Spanish literature, and he may have known Tirso. A definite answer to the question might be arrived at by a study of Pushkin's letters and other Russian material.

The romantic poets of many lands gave new life to Don Juan and interpreted his character in terms of their own philosophies of life and their individual tastes. Of these later conceptions, Pushkin seems to have been most stirred by Mozart's opera *Don Giovanni*. The libretto for this opera was written by that Italian adventurer (friend of Casanova) da Ponte. His source was Italian, but he may well have put something of himself into his hero. Pushkin quotes on the frontispiece of his

Stone Guest the lines which Leporello the servant in the opera addresses to the statue:

> "O statua gentilissima
> Del gran Commendatore! . . .
> Ah, perdoni!"

and he names the servant of Don Juan, Leporello.

If there are at times suggestions of Goethe's *Faust,* one is not surprised, and one thinks involuntarily of the days when these two great figures of legend, Don Juan and Dr. Faustus, by their horrible ends edified the audiences of the puppet plays in Germany.

Of the lyric beauty of Pushkin's version of *Don Juan* nothing can be said by a person lacking a knowledge of Russian. The Bodenstedt translation into German, however, gives one a sense of the charm which must be there, and which, it seems to me, the English translator has been unable to pass on to his readers.

"Faust is the greatest creation of the poetic spirit; it represents present day poetry, as the Iliad is typical of the classic past." (1827).
—*Alexander Pushkin.*

VIII

Excerpt from Boris Brasol's
THE MIGHTY THREE

V

I awoke one morning, and found myself famous.
                                    BYRON

POUSHKIN was only twenty when he completed *Ruslán and Ludmíla,* a light and fanciful poem which, though fully expressive of his boyish sentiments, made his name famous overnight.

For the first time in Russian literary annals, the epic element and mythical themes were made the basis of, and freely interwoven with, a poetic composition of this kind. By one stroke of his pen, Poushkin swept into discard a long standing tradition of verbose and pretentious pseudo-classicism. With remarkable ease, he threw open the treasury of Slavic Epos, and suddenly, its colorful characters and symbols, like gushing Spring cascades, poured into the well of Russian aesthetic meditations.

Ruslán and Ludmíla was so astoundingly new

in form and so profoundly popular in substance that it instantly focussed general attention on its young author, who, hitherto, had been admired chiefly as a brilliant minstrel of love, anacreontic in his leanings and epicurean in his tastes.

The Prologue, which Poushkin added to the poem several years after its completion, strikes just the right keynote of *Ruslán and Ludmíla,* with these two lines resounding as its overture and finale chords:

> "Affairs of long departed days,
>   Of olden times undying legends."

The mysteries of the Russian fairy world unroll in this prelude—which is only an airy sketch, as it were, a casual touch of the artist's brush—vividly suggesting the theme and variations of the story which Poushkin tells in perfect rhymes. This is the synthetic picture drawn by the poet in his Prologue:

> "A seashore oak 'neath magic skies
>   Swings from its boughs a golden chain,
>   And day and night, Sir Cat the Wise
>   Walks back and forth this fairy lane.
>   He purrs a song, when to his right
>   He turns; when to his left—a tale;
>   'Tis Wonderland! There dwells a Sprite;
>   Old Nick roams there; this is his trail;
>   There, wonder beasts on wood paths hide
>   And track the forests o'er and o'er;
>   A hut stands there, hens' legs astride,

Without a window or a door;
There, vales are full of ghosts forlorn;
There, waves embrace the shore at morn,—
The sandy shore, all desolate,—
And thirty knights, all bold and fair,
Rise from the waters, pair by pair,
And with them comes their old sea-mate;
A Royal Prince, with playful ease,
Enslaves a Czar of awing might;
There, 'midst the clouds, o'er woods and seas,
Old Wizard, in the people's sight,
With anger drags a valiant knight;
A Princess grieves in prison there,
The Brown Wolf serving her with care;
There, by itself, a Cauldron rambles
With Old-Witch roving through the brambles;
There,—gold is heaped; Kaschéy rots near it;
That's Russia, that is Russian spirit! . . .
And I roamed there, along those trails,
I saw the oak 'neath magic skies,
And there I sat, while Cat the Wise
Was purring me his wonder tales.

I still remember one he told:
List! while I let this tale unfold."

And the tale takes us back to the happy days of Prince Wladímir—"the Golden Sun"—the beloved hero in Russian legend and folk song. We see him, shining in his brocade attire, amidst a gorgeous feast which he is giving at his Kiev Palace in honor of Ludmíla, his youngest daughter, who has just become the bride of Ruslán—a valiant and undaunted knight.

Three rivals of the princely groom are attending the merry celebration—Rogdaí, a flaming, fearless warrior; Farláf, an uppish bawler,

> "At feasts, unconquered and unrivalled,
> But modest in the face of glaives",

and Ratmír, a youthful Khasar Khan,

> "All three, quite pale and rather gloomy—
> To them the feast is not a feast."

Says Poushkin:

> "Our ancestors ate long and slowly,
> And slowly did they move around."

Many a song has been sung, many a dish emptied, many a pitcher of mead consumed, before the noisy revel came to its drowsy end. Now, at last, Ruslán can escort Ludmíla to their bedroom. . . . And soon silence reigns throughout the Palace.

Suddenly, with lightning and thunder, a dark cloud descends upon the castle; all lights are blown out, and amidst horror and amazement, Ludmíla is swept away by some mysterious ghost.

Overwhelmed with grief, Prince Wladímir solemnly promises to give Ludmíla to him who finds her and safely brings her back. Ruslán and the three other claimants of the beautiful Princess, each take an oath that they will rescue and restore her to the stricken father.

Then comes the thrilling Odyssey of innumerable adventures which the four knights experience during their perilous wanderings through Kingdoms near and far in search of Ludmíla. Fate miraculously favors Ruslán, and finally, he does learn that Ludmíla was carried away and enslaved by cruel Chernomór, a long-bearded Wizard, dwelling in some remote dominion. Desperate are Ruslán's struggles, hazardous his encounters with daring enemies and unyielding Nature. But success crowns his venture, and he finds his beloved bride in Chernomór's enchanted castle; he captures the cruel Wizard and, filled with happiness and joy, he brings Ludmíla back to Kiev, while Chernomór, stripped of his magic beard, deprived of his dark power, and now but a humble dwarf, is presented by Ruslán to Wladímir, who makes him a trusted page at his brilliant Court. Reunited, Ruslán and Ludmíla celebrate the happy end of their calamities and troubles. Such is the mirthful conclusion of Poushkin's joyous story:

> "Affairs of long departed days,
> Of olden times undying legends...."

Ruslán and Ludmíla was the first original creation of Russian romanticism. Hitherto, in strict adherence to Schiller's and Uhland's fashion, fantastic topics were usually associated with sagas of Western mediævalism, and to this extent, they were purely imitative. With his instinctive longing for the national ideal, Poushkin refused to borrow alien material for the expression of a romantic dream, and so he deliberately turned to Russian epics. There, he discovered a whole world of strange images and reanimating colors, and these he masterfully brought in harmony with the fancies of his own creative imagination. Of this accord a brilliant work of art was born.

Russian men of letters greeted *Ruslán* with almost unanimous applause. They all stressed the beauty of its style and the fresh richness of its poetic tongue.

Yet Poushkin himself, with his sense of superior refinement, was not in the least pleased with the poem, and in a letter to Prince Viazemsky, dating back to that period, he stated:

> "I finished my poem, but only the last, or final, verse gave me genuine satisfaction. . . . I am so bored with it that I simply cannot make up my mind to copy it, though by fragments, for you."

And in a subsequent note he made the defiant remark:

> "*Ruslán* is but a suckling."

Also, in the text of the poem itself, Poushkin bestows upon his creation various belittling epithets, such as "funny story", "light nonsense", "mirthful labor," and "sinful songs."

Indirectly, the same sentiment of discontent is intimated in the Epilogue to *Ruslán:*

> "In vain I long for fascination:
> They faded—my poetic dreams,
> The days of love and golden beams,
> The days of happy meditation.
> Ye fleeted, moments of delight,
> And thou hast vanished out of sight—
> Oh, Muse of cadenced inspiration."

Surely Poushkin must have felt—and later this was correctly observed by several Russian critics—that, despite the popular style in which *Ruslán and Ludmíla* was written, he had not yet completely freed himself from Western standards: Here and there, particularly in the technique of Poushkin's verse, one does notice the influence upon him of poets like Voltaire and Ariosto.

But while *Ruslán* should not be conceived as an altogether independent product of Russian literary thought, it did prove the turning point in the history of Poushkin's own artistic growth. From that time on, foreign patterns were never taken by him as something granted; he pondered over them with veneration, as one should over any noble achievement of the human mind; he absorbed the ideas of the great European masters, but then his mighty genius would remint, remelt, reintegrate their dreams and visions into strikingly novel forms and astounding revelations.

VI

> *This morning I conversed with Russia's most remarkable man.*
>
> > Emperor Nicholas I (after his interview with Poushkin)
>
> *La critique est aisée—l'art est difficile.*

The early creations of Poushkin, not excluding his *Ruslán,* as much as the whimsical arabesques interlaced with the bucolic motives of his lyre, were largely responsible for a legend which, temporarily at least, did cast a doubt on the scope and breadth of our poet's creative achievements. Shortly after his death, stories began to be told about the alleged "giddiness of the Poushkin talent"—a myth which, in days past, has been fancifully flourishing in the critical columns of many a leading magazine.

Only gradually, step by step, the Russians grew conscious of the fact that there is in Poushkin, in addition to frivolity and mirth, innate mischief and incurable optimism, graceful lightness and joyous animation—another aspect, an almost unsuspected phase of his mental make-up which, for a long time, has been sadly overlooked by both the poet's admirers and censors, but which, today, we unhesitatingly acknowledge as his *profound wisdom.*

Certainly, Gogol was right when, as far back as in 1832, he said:

"Poushkin is an extraordinary, and perhaps unique, phenomenon of the Russian spirit: he represents the Russian in his development, such as he may become in some two hundred years. In Poushkin, the Russian nature, the Russian soul, the Russian tongue, the Russian character are reflected in such purity, in such refined beauty, as a landscape mirrored on the convex surface of an optical glass."

The serene philosophy of Poushkin; the Homeric calmness of his world outlook; his sane Hellenic approach to the earnest problems which persistently weigh upon man's conscience,—all this was particularly surprising at the threshold of the general decline of European culture—on the eve of Schopenhauer's metaphysical pessimism, Flaubert's aesthetic nihilism, Baudelaire's pathological sensualism, Nietzsche's rebellious anarchism, and Maeterlinck's mystical symbolism.

Poushkin was preëminently a poet of this World and not of the Next; he loved life, but he embraced it in its entirety,

"Without repentant aches, without distressing doubts,
Without faint-hearted tears at parting with the earth."

Perhaps, not in a strictly gnosiological, but certainly in an aesthetic and cultural sense, the wisdom of Poushkin, like priceless pearls, is scattered through his many poems and lyrical verses; tragedies and studies of the Russian folk lore; letters and prose fragments; critical essays and historical works, but particularly, in his virtuosic conversations, which Olga Smirnóva, as Eckermann in the case of Goethe, recorded with loving care.

In her illustrious salon, Poushkin reigned supreme. When he spoke, everybody kept silent. And there was no end to his brilliant discourses on history, religion, science, literature, politics, philosophy and art. Those who had been watching Poushkin's phenomenal mental growth, were unable to comprehend when and how he found time to absorb such an immense volume of diversified knowledge as he revealed in his undying talks.

This, for instance, is a typical passage from Poushkin's monologues:

"Why did Plato seek to banish art from his Republic? This is illogical. . . . He says that Beauty is the luster of Truth; to this I add that Beauty should be the luster of Good. I will show you a fragment from one of the Neo-Platonics—I do not recall his name: Beauty, Truth and Symmetry are expressions of the Supreme Being. . . . Still, the Platonists failed to achieve the Beautiful, which is equivalent to Good translated into deed; they were merely dreaming of attaining that aim. Only Christianity succeeded in bringing about this accord. Perfect beauty is, to put it in one word, —*Harmony,* and what can be more lucid and more majestic than Harmony?—Joukovsky is right when he says that the Beauty of the Dreadful amounts to sacrilege."

On another occasion, speaking of English philosophy, Poushkin commented:

"I was reading Locke, and I found that his is a religious mind, but one which confines knowledge to the feasible, though he himself had stated that in matters of faith the Bible, more than anything else, teaches us the truth, and that all problems of religious belief, while exceeding reason, do not contradict it. . . . Finally, I came to the conviction that man found God precisely because He exists. It is impossible, even in the world of plastical forms, to discover anything that does not exist—a thought which was conveyed to me by Art. . . . A form cannot be devised: it has to be derived from something that actually is. Nor is it possible to invent sentiments, thoughts and ideas not planted in us, those having a common root with the mysterious instinct which distinguishes a creature who at once feels and reasons, from that which merely feels. This reality is as real as everything that we can touch, experience or behold. The people possess an innate longing for this kind of reality—the religious sentiment—which they even refuse to analyze. Religion created art and literature, in fact, everything that was great in ancient times. Everything is dependent upon the religious feeling . . . and without it there would have been no philosophy, no poetry, no ethics."

With equal facility our poet would learnedly discuss Aristotle and the *Novum Organum,* Pascal's *Thoughts* and the theological principles of

Calvinism; Ptolemaic astronomy and English history; the Newtonian system and the songs of the minnesingers. To Poushkin, the world of knowledge was just as much an open book as Nature herself, with which, like Goethe, he breathed a life in common.

Yet, *"nul n'est prophète dans son pays"*.... The greatness of Poushkin, though recognized by his contemporaries, was vehemently challenged by the half-nihilistic or quasi-positivistic faction of Russian public opinion under Alexander II.

In the Sixties', Dmitry Pissarev, the eloquent but vainglorious apologist of materialism, started the anti-Poushkin crusade. His attack was followed by a series of others which were kept up over a period of several decades.

No doubt, there must have been something in the character of Poushkin, in his philosophy, in the complex gamut of his ideas and innate leanings that explains, though does not justify in the least, the conspicuous one-sidedness in the evaluation of his creative work by men of the Pissarev school.

To these Slavic apostles of Western radicalism, and through them—to the whole pleiad of the Russians who, during the Epoch of the Great Reforms, were chewing the cud of crude biological dogmatism, Poushkin was objectionable on the mere ground that his poetry was a glorious emblem of elegance and self-contained harmony. But the shaggy critics of those days ridiculed pure lyricism, and blamed Poushkin for having set an example to a whole progeny of poets, who were old-fashioned enough to admire Shakespeare in poetry, Chopin—in music, Raphael—in painting, and for whom Beauty, Love and Nature still retained both charm and value. Yet Pissarev neither could understand nor would forgive art devoid of some didactic, but preferably political, purpose, and he had no use for all the Petrarchs with their Lauras, the aesthetes, the Fets, indulging in the delicate weaving of verbless rhymes such as these:

> "Murmurs. Breezes. Trills and singing
> Of the nightingale.
> Silver touches, gentle swinging
> O'er the drowsy vale.
>
> Lights and shadows. Strange sensations.
> Visions full of grace,
> And the magic of mutations
> In that lovely face.
>
> Clouds in purple. Amber blushes
> 'Cross the misty lawn!
> Tears and kisses. Sudden flushes!
> And the dawn! The dawn!"

Poushkin once said that he "preferred verses without a plan, rather than a plan without verses." However, the dull Catos of Russian literary manners, insisted that poetry should serve some utilitarian purpose, prosaic though it be. And how they hated the "murmurs" and "breezes"! For them Rouget de Lisle was the greatest among all poets, and

> *"Allons enfants, de la patrie!—*
> *Le jour de gloire est arrivé"*

the finest kind of poetry.

In their view inspiration of the Poushkin order was a glaring symptom of inexcusable lightmindedness. They who sought to establish equations between a keg of nails and the *Moonlight Sonata,* between a yard of cloth and a Keats' Sonnet,—they were utterly unwilling and unable to forgive Poushkin the ineffable aristocratism of his spirit, his sincere aversion to human vulgarism, which J. S. Mill caustically labelled "conglomerated mediocrity", and which to both Gogol and Dostoievsky became the everlasting denominator of Evil itself.

Poushkin's distaste for the democratic ideal and the dogmas of loose liberalism was the outgrowth of a whole life philosophy, the truth of which only now, in the Twentieth Century, begins to be surmised by sociologists and thinkers of the more constructive orientation.

A keen student of history, Poushkin knew that social progress is rarely, if ever, the result of mass action and mob rule, but rather the fruit of creative genius, the function of the individual's prudent intervention in the course of human affairs.

"At all times,"—says Poushkin—"mankind was governed by the enlightened will . . . of the few. . . . Under all forms of government, men inevitably submitted themselves to the minority, or to the individual, so that, in a sense, the term 'democracy' appears to me meaningless and void of foundation. . . . Owing to the differences in talents and even physical constitution, there is no uniformity among human beings, and therefore, there is no equality. For the reformation of Russia the force of Peter alone proved sufficient. Napoleon, with no help from outside, muzzled the remnants of the Revolution. . . . The masses followed these men and supported them, but the first word was always spoken by them. All this stands in direct contradiction to the democratic system which tolerates not the leadership of individuals, and yet, they go to make up the natural aristocracy. . . . I doubt whether the world will ever see the end of that which springs out of the depths of the human mind, and which prevails in Nature herself,—I mean, *inequality*."

These principles determined Poushkin's irreconcilable attitude towards the mob, kicking, with its democratic hoof, at the heraldic lion.

Speaking, in a letter to Prince Viazemsky, of Byron's "Memoirs", Poushkin expressed this interesting thought:

"The rabble is avid to read confessions, reminiscences, etc., because, in their meanness, they rejoice over the humiliations of the noble and the weaknesses of the mighty. Whenever they discover infamy of some kind, they feel delighted: 'Aha, he is as little as we, and he is just as abominable as we are!' But you are lying, shameful wretches: he is both little and abominable, but not like you—differently."

Time and again, Poushkin reiterated his repugnance for the vulgar, which does play such a manifest part in human affairs. In the *Monument,* which is Poushkin's own Requiem, he says:

> "Nay, I shall not completely die; in sacred strains
> My soul survives my dust; forever is its worth.
> And famous shall I be, so long as there remains
> A single Poet on this earth.
> . . . .
> By God's command, O Muse, abide obediently,
> Nor shalt thou dread reproach, nor claim the
>   Poet's bay:
> To praise and blame alike thou shouldst indifferent be,
> And let the fool have his own say."

The same note sounds in Poushkin's poem *The Rabble,* with its proud epigraph: *"Procul este, profani",* whose concluding four lines

> "Not for earthly agitation,
>   Not for gain or battle grounds,—
> We are born for inspiration,
>   Rev'rend prayers and sweet sounds",

in the past, caused a violent storm of indignation in radical quarters, and which even in our day seem to weigh upon the over-sensitive conscience of the professional propagators of the revolutionary gospel.

VII

Mortem effugere nemo potest
CICERO

Let Sun live forever!
Let gloom disappear!
POUSHKIN

MUCH has been said and written about Poushkin's so-called "Byronism". No doubt, the sense of aristocratic superiority, inherent in our poet, was akin to Byron's disdainful attitude towards everything that has no right or claim, whether imaginary or real, to immortality. Still, the inception of Poushkin's protestant moods is to be sought not so much in the contemptuous opinions of the disillusioned Lord as in the skeptical witticisms of the French *causeurs* and thinkers who, by their pens and tongues, paved the way for the drama of 1789. But even unassisted by Voltaire and Diderot, young Poushkin quickly grasped *le ridicule* in Russian every-day life; for this he had only to invoke his penetrating sense of humor which, later, he imparted to Gogol. But Gogol's sarcasm degenerated into that form of wit which, Hazlitt tells us, is so applied to given objects "as to make the little look less, the mean more light and worthless." This tendency in Gogol gradually assumed a pathological course, culminating in satirical hyperbolism. The innate feeling of measure and proportion guarded Poushkin against any such leanings.

Yet, when one is green, it does seem delightful to be challenging the whole universe and advocating immediate revaluation of all values. Before having read a single line from *Manfred* or from *Cain,* Poushkin wrote, in succession, a naughty ode to *Freedom,* and an inspired little poem *The Village,* in which he passionately and nobly denounced serfdom. But above all, he enjoyed making fun of that which is funny, and his caustic epigrams, applauded as they were in the camp of his partisans and bottle-mates, provoked bitter indignation among his enemies and grudgers.

In the early part of the Nineteenth Century, Russia, in more than one way, was still a crude country, and as any other country, she had her own prominent fools and influential philisters, displaying their distasteful self-conceit. And Poushkin simply could not desist from attacking those inflated guardians of public morals who earnestly believed that their reputation, like that of Cæsar's wife, was beyond reproach.

Finally, the poet did get himself in trouble, and

in 1820, he was ordered to leave the capital for the South, ostensibly in connection with a government mission of some sort.

This "exile" brought Poushkin to the Caucasus, with its grandiose scenery, war-like spirit, and romantic atmosphere. It was only there that Poushkin began to take an interest in Byron, that sovereign of European thought, who "suffered, loved and damned", as our poet himself put it.

There was one aspect in Byron which particularly appealed to the rising genius of Russia: The Britisher hated conventions of every kind, and so did Poushkin. Both experienced fervent passion for freedom, and both despised hypocrisy, that traditional fig leaf of vice and evil. But even during his Byronic period, the Russian poet evinced remarkable latitude of thought and independence of opinion.

In Poushkin's intellectual diapason, Byron was but one of the many links, and the creator of *Childe Harold* never did succeed in depriving the merry little "Cricket" of his own original and self-reliant way. Besides, the humorous flavor, so pronounced in Poushkin, was almost non-existent in the British poet.

Byron was too rebellious to be free; Poushkin was too free to become rebellious. Byron damned, while Poushkin blessed this earth of ours. Byron suffered, but he would have been even more unhappy without his sufferings and sorrows; Poushkin suffered, too, but the theme of egocentric grief never could have made him happy. In Byron the element of challenge was a symptom of some fatal inner discord; in Poushkin, the impulsive protest was always mitigated by an inveterate longing for undisturbed harmony.

The pacific strain, indeed, was the dominant note of Poushkin's moral credo. Ever since his Lyceum days, he had been impressed with the ancient Hellenic tradition—an order of things which was primarily based upon the principles of rhythm and beauty. Naturally, he began to conceive life itself as a harmonic whole, of which art, to him, was but the loftiest manifestation. This balanced philosophy, so cardinally different from that of Byron's, made Poushkin immune to bitter disillusions and that gloomy frame of mind which sometimes is spoken of as "negativism."

Man's stoic approach to the enigma of Death is the surest touchstone of his deep penetration into the mystery of Life. In his own conduct, subconsciously, Poushkin seems to have been always influenced by Seneca's rigorous maxim: *"Long for the inevitable."* Fond as Poushkin was of this earthly existence, he never dreaded Death—the fatal end of all beginning.

At the age of seventeen, he paints this picture:

"Clear will come life's parting hours,
And our maiden playmates bright

THE MIGHTY THREE

Will collect our ashes light
Into feast urns, crowned with flowers."

The same sentiment, only in a humorous vein, was voiced by the poet, when he was thirty, in a letter to Pletnév, a Lyceum friend of his:

"Look out! Spleen is more dangerous than cholera: Cholera kills merely the flesh, while spleen poisons the soul. Délvig died. Molchánov passed away. Wait,—Joukovsky will also die, and we will be dead, too. But life is still rich; we shall meet newcomers, and contract new friendships. Your daughter will grow, and will become engaged. We will turn into old dotards, and our wives—into old hags. But our children will be lovely, young and merry scamps; the boys will be engaged in mischief, the girls—the little rascals—will indulge in sentimentalism, and the sight of them will make us joyous. Nonsense, my dear: Nothing matters, so long as we live, and the day may come when, again, we shall be glad and happy."

Even more impressively Poushkin revealed this basic attitude toward life and death in his world-renowned *Stanzas:*

"When, through the noisy streets I'm strolling,
  Or 'mid the thoughtless rabble-streams,
Or where the temple-bells are tolling,—
  I give myself unto my dreams.

I say: the years are swiftly flying,
  We soon no longer shall appear,

In rest, beneath the death vault lying:
　For some—the hour is drawing near.

I view yon oak with veneration,
　And think: this patriarch, in his prime,
Will yet outlive my generation,
　As he outlived my father's time.

And when a sweet babe I'm caressing,
　I think: I go to give thee room;
I look on thee with farewell blessing:
　'Tis mine to fade, and thine to bloom.

And ev'ry day and year I ponder
　On what the future has in store;
What season will it be, I wonder,
　When I shall pass and be no more?
. . . .

Where'er my senseless frame reposes,
　When it decays, it cannot care,
Yet I would rest 'mid springing roses,
　I fain would lie where all is fair.

Let fresh young life be ever playing
　Around the portal of my tomb,
Let Nature ever be displaying
　Her careless charm, her fadeless bloom." *

It is doubtful whether Byron could have written a reconciled poem such as this. . . .

And only three weeks before his death, Poushkin dedicated to his wife these few lines in which, again, he emphasized his calm and sedate realization of the inevitable:

* English version by Lindsay S. Perkins.

" 'Tis time, my friend, 'tis time! For peace my
   heart is striving:
Time flies, days fade away, and ev'ry day is
   driving
Us nearer to the fatal end. But you and I—
We plan to live. Alas, some day we have to die.
Not happiness, but peace, is life's most ardent
   quest.
There now dwells but one desire in my breast:
As some exhausted slave, I dream of taking
   flight
To distant realms of harmony and pure delight."

Dostoievsky reflected much upon the grave problems with which mankind has always to contend, but he sadly failed to find the bridge between this world and the next. He was unable to comprehend the truth—so clearly understood by Poushkin—that Death is merely the eternal shadow and inseparable companion of everlasting Life. Dostoievsky's heroes are constantly tormented by the ghost of the Grim Reaper, and, like Flaubert, they are haunted by the sinister thought that visible and measurable reality is a veil, only here and there, covering the cold and silent continuity of Death. This fixed idea, like the majestically mournful leitmotiv of Tchaikovsky's Sixth Symphony, permeates all their somber rovings.

So it was also with Tolstoy: The more he had been thinking of Death; the more he had kept urging others not to be afraid of it,—the farther he departed from the only possible, genuinely Poushkin, and classically simple solution of the Sphinx's eternal riddle.

Amongst George Watts' most famous canvases there is one called "Love and Death". With intense pathos he portrays the idea—for his preëminently is ideographic art—of the tragic essence of inescapable Destiny: At the threshold of a human dwelling, Cupid, with his little hand extended, seeks in vain to arrest the march of inflexible Fate or Death. Only one obstacle stands between him and Life—"There Inside", one faint barrier—Love, that faithful companion of a heart intoxicated with happiness. The dreadful Guest has not yet reached the door. But in another fleeting moment he will enter the morose chamber, and the song of Love will be forever stilled, and the flame of Life will impotently die, and there will be Darkness.

Virtually all Russian writers, with the one exception of Poushkin, seem to have been oppressed by the foreboding of triumphant death. No doubt, this feeling, whether indirectly or otherwise, was born out of Byron's songs of universal grief and the sighs of his lamenting lyre. But sullen pessimism was utterly alien to Poushkin: Throughout his whole life, brief though it was, he has been guided by that vital urge for serene calmness of the spirit, which was the source of his sunny dreams and lucid inspiration.

VIII

The quality of mercy is not strain'd. ...
                                    SHAKESPEARE

WHAT is termed as Poushkin's Byronism was chiefly confined to his critical estimation of the psycho-social merits, or intrinsic value, of civilization. In *The Caucasian Captive, The Bakhchisaraï Fountain* and *The Gypsies*—the three principal poems relating to the Russian poet's Byronic period, he sought to ascertain the specific gravity of human progress devoid of spiritual refinement and culture. Does, indeed, civilization make for individual betterment of man, and does it tend to uplift his soul?

These questions Poushkin answered in the negative.

Tired of the monotony of civilized life, Aleko, the hero of *The Gypsies,* departs for the steppes of Bessarabia, and there, among the half-savage Bohemian tribes, he struggles to find a "new freedom". In this he fails emphatically because the deeply imbedded social prejudices retain a firm grip on him; he mistakes freedom for license, and he imposes his despotic will upon a community of peaceful nomads.

To this extent, Aleko's revolt against the irksome conventions of what Rousseau called the *"contrat social"*, is superficial and formal; it does not go to the bottom of things, nor does it strike at the sources of commonplace morality. On the contrary, his ethical code, though revolutionary in appearance, is that of an averagely well-meaning bourgeois, in whom the property instinct, though latent, is often the governing motive of his every-day conduct. But to the primitive races, the generic notion of *jus utendi et abutendi,* that all-pervading principle of Roman law, is altogether alien and unknown.

Gypsy psychology is that of a happy little bird singing his carefree hymns to the blue sky and the golden Sun. Poushkin tells us of these placid moods in verses full of loveliness and unaffected charm:

> "God's wee birdie is not grieving,
> Knowing neither toil nor care,
> And a nest he is not weaving
> That shall weather lasting wear.
> On the bough, the long night dreaming,
> Shakes the dewdrops from his wings,
> And when morn's red sun is beaming,
> Hears the voice of God and sings.
> After lovely Spring, the Summer
> Brings the days of glowing heat;
> Autumn then, a later comer,
> Ushers in the fog and sleet.
> Men are pining, men are grieving;
> O'er the sea, with tireless wing,
> Birdie for the South is leaving,
> Flying onward to the Spring." *

* English version by Lindsay S. Perkins.

THE MIGHTY THREE 125

The impending conflict between Aleko, the haughty offshoot of self-conceited society, and the gypsies, those humble sons of virginal Nature, culminates in a complete and stormy break between the two.

Aleko, when talking to Zemfíra, the Bohemian girl with whom he falls in love, eloquently denounces "civilization"; he scoffs at the slavery of those who belong to the educated strata. According to him, crowded cities, the living emblems of our age, are unbearable:

> "Men live fenced in like cattle there;
> They do not breathe the morning air,
> Nor do they scent the meadows sweet.
> They are ashamed to love, to think;
> They sell their freedom, dull their brains,
> Before their idols cringe and sink,—
> They long for money and for chains."

Still, Aleko himself proves a captive of blind egoism, and this vice he inherits from that very society which he professes to despise. He loves Zemfíra, and, for a short while, she also takes a fancy to him. But free is a gypsy's heart: it loves just as long as it whims, and it will be guided by no imposed precepts or formal restraint. To Aleko, this is beyond comprehension: he seeks to make the sentiment of emotion subject to the law of property just as much as any merchandise displayed in a shop window. The abrupt finale is reached when

Zemfíra becomes infatuated with one of her young tribesmen. She then turns away from Aleko as naturally and freely as she had given herself to him, and our hero, in a wild outburst of jealousy and wrath, kills his self-willed and unfaithful sweetheart.

The dramatic effect of Aleko's deed is made still more graphic by the concluding monologue of Zemfíra's father, who, in a purely Poushkin fashion, takes a forgiving attitude towards the murderer of his daughter. In the mind of the old Bohemian, individual freedom cannot exist alongside blood and terror. And so, instead of taking revenge against Aleko, he merely orders him to leave the camp, where true liberty and undisturbed peace are the only laws by which everybody must abide. And he says:

> . . . .
> "Do leave us, self-conceited man!
> We're wild and have no use for laws,
> We punish not, we torture not,
> We dread the sight of bloody claws,
> And we won't share a slayer's lot.
> . . . .
> Farewell, depart from us in peace!"

The merciful hand of Poushkin never strikes an enemy that is no longer menacing. Despite his cruel crime, Aleko is crushed by his own vain passion. He will return to those sad realms where men, "like cattle", are herded in the prisons of modern civilization. This will be his punishment, his doom.

Such is Poushkin's philosophy always. One more example suffices: In 1821, Napoleon expired in exile on the island of St. Helena. He was Russia's most formidable enemy, and his invasion shook the mighty Empire to its foundations. How did Poushkin react to the passing of that dishonored favorite of Fortune?—To him he dedicated a poem full of eulogy and compassion. Its last eight lines give a magnificent proof of the greatness of our poet's soul:

> "But shame and curses without number
> Upon that reptile head be laid,
> Whose senseless blame shall vex the slumber
> Of him—that sad discrownèd shade!
> Praised be! He showed the Russian nation
> Their lofty fate, and even stilled,
> From exile's gloom, for man's elation,
> Eternal liberty he willed." *

Again, here, a bitter discord resulting from the historical strife between two elemental forces, Napoleon and Russia, resolves itself into a soothing accord.

In this way Poushkin overcomes the Byronic disease, emerging from the turmoil of his inner doubts and struggles as a great master of all-conquering harmony.

* First four lines, with corrections, taken from Thomas B. Shaw's English version of Poushkin's poem *Napoleon*.

IX

Not every Perugino can claim a Raphael as his disciple.

OSTRACISED from the two capitals, in 1824, Poushkin was still journeying in Southern Russia. On several occasions before, his political reputation had been questioned by the omniscient police of those days and, while living in Odessa, Poushkin again invoked upon himself the displeasure of the Government: Accused of "bad behavior", but more particularly, of having made a casual atheistic remark, Poushkin was ordered to leave the Black Sea metropolis and to retire to Mikháilovskoie, his own estate in the Province of Pskov. He arrived at this new station of his exile in the Autumn of the same year, and there he dwelt fully twenty-four weary months.

Much as the enforced sojourn in provincial seclusion was annoying, it proved extremely beneficial to the mental development and artistic achievements of our poet. In rustication, he undertook a serious study of Shakespeare and Russian history. It was then that he conceived one of his *opera magna*—the tragedy *Borís Godounóv*.

This work in Poushkin's creative life proved a definite departure from subjective lyricism. Here, he resigned his individuality in favor of historical objectivism. For a lyrical poet *par excellence,* a feat such as this must be considered a signal victory which, in the case of Poushkin, became the stepping stone to his subsequent literary triumphs.

In devising the plan of *Borís Godounóv,* Poushkin, emulating Shakespeare's example, eliminated the entire etiquette and pedantry of conventional pseudo-classicism. Very justly, the Russian poet perceived the greatest glory of Shakespeare in his sagacious understanding of the human soul, with all its shifting moods, subdued longings, tempered and untempered passions, vexing doubts, mad jealousies, overwhelming hatreds, and triumphant love. Out of these elements Shakespeare's dramas were carved for eternity, and it is upon this material that the dynamics of his plays, their plots and conflicts, were conditioned.

Poushkin himself was graced with a keen dramatic sense and an almost instinctive ability to conjecture the approaching cataclysm of two colliding passions—that impact which is the inevitable result of two active forces mutually challenging each other.

In the arrangement of the scenes Poushkin adopted Shakespeare's architectural freedom and his disregard for any ossified rules on the place and time of the action. It was also under the influence of the British dramatist that Poushkin introduced in his play blank verse in artful combination with prose. No one in Russia before Poushkin resorted to this mixed style in which *Borís Godounóv* was moulded.

Apparently, Poushkin was satisfied with his new work:

> "I congratulate you, my darling," he wrote to Viazemsky—"upon a romantic tragedy, in which Borís Godounóv is the leading character. My tragedy is completed. I read it over to myself aloud and started clapping my hands and exclaiming: 'Look at Poushkin! Isn't he clever!'"

The problem which Poushkin had set out to solve was, indeed, a difficult one: he sought to reveal in his creation the true atmosphere of the early part of the Seventeenth Century, which, in Russian history, is known as "The Confused Period". In the whole gallery of its actors, Czar Borís himself was the most enigmatic and momentous figure: A man of humble descent and Tartar extraction, Borís, in his struggle for supremacy—first, under John the Terrible, and later, under his weakling son, Czar Fëdor—had lived through a trying school of court intrigues, endless envy and political reverses.

Boundlessly ambitious, Borís, in his thoughts and actions, was constantly guided by one dominant motive—his passionate desire to ascend the Throne. Even before becoming Czar of Russia, and while Fëdor was still reigning, Godounóv attained dictatorial power. But Fëdor had an adolescent brother, Dmitry, who was to have been his lawful successor. That child stood as an insurmountable obstacle to Godounóv's cherished goal.

One day Dmitry was found mysteriously murdered in a town not far from Moscow. At once, the hundred-mouthed goddess started spreading rumors that Boris had inspired the murder. But from that time on, his road to the Crown of Russia was clear and now he could be patiently awaiting Fëdor's natural death. Meanwhile, Godounóv kept watching and scrutinizing his Sovereign's character, cleverly using to his own advantage the Czar's kind-hearted disposition, with all its indecision and morbid meekness.

Count Alexis Tolstoy, in his tragedy *Czar Fëdor Ioánnovich,* brilliantly contrasted the domineering character of Borís with Fëdor's weak and apathetic temper. Says Godounóv:

"A mountain, huge and high,
Was Czar Iván. The subterranean shocks,
From its tenebrous depths, would shake the plain,
Or, from its peak, a sudden burst of flame
Would cast upon the earth both death and ruin.
Czar Fëdor is not thus. I would compare
Him rather with a cleft in open field:
The crevices and porous ground about
Are carefully concealed by flowers in the grass.
Incautiously, when wandering near by,
The shepherd and the herd slip down the pit.
A legend lives amongst our village folk:
It is believed that long ago a church

Had sunk into the earth, and on that spot,
A hollow—huge and dark—had formed itself;
And people say that when the sky is clear,
And calm prevails, from down below, soft sounds
Of pealing bells are sometimes heard.
As holy, but as treacherous a place,
Appears to me Czar Fëdor. In his soul,
Which stays wide open to both foe and friend,
There always dwell, as gentle melodies
Of chiming bells, sweet prayers, love and mercy.
And yet, what good is all this clemency,
Indeed, what good is it—without foundation?
'Tis now seven years since Czar Iván
Has swept o'er Russia like a mighty storm.
For seven years, with greatest care and pain,
Stone after stone, I have been daily building
That edifice; that great and sacred temple;
That potent state; that new and prudent country;
That Russia, so beloved by me, whose fate
Absorbs my thoughts through weary, sleepless
    nights.
In vain! ... With sorrow do I feel that I
Am building over an abyss, and suddenly,
That edifice may crumble, for the humblest
Among my enemies, of his volition,
Can sway the Sov'reign's meek and tender heart,
Uprooting those desires which I inspire."

Fëdor having died, Borís was soon proclaimed Czar of Russia. In Poushkin's tragedy, he becomes the focal figure around which, treachery, intrigues, jealousies and hatreds, begin to weave. The rumor of Dmitry's mysterious death suggests to a young impostor, an obscure monk in the Chóudov

Monastery, the daring plot of assuming the name and title of the slain boy. The pseudo-Czarevich flees to Poland, and there he convinces the grandees that he is Dmitry, who had been miraculously saved from the hands of Godounóv's hirelings. The ghost of the martyred youth menacingly looms in the dark background of popular discontent spreading throughout troubled Russia.

The climax of the tragedy comes almost at the beginning of the play: Already in his second appearance the Czar divulges the secret of his mortifying distress. Even at this early stage one can discern the sounds *funèbres* of the wrathful hymn:

> "*Dies irae, dies illa!*
> *Solvet saeclum in favilla.*
> *Judex ergo cum sedebit—*
> *Quidquid latet, adparebit,*
> *Nil inultum remanebit.*"

This theme of expiation is preëminently Poushkin's; he constantly reverts to the strange law of retribution, which to Dostoievsky is the source of man's inner punishment.

In an impressive monologue Godounóv ponders over the real cause of his psychic malady. He says:

> "I did ascend to sovereign power.
> It is six years, or nearly so, that I
> Am reigning peacefully, and yet, my soul
> Of happiness remains devoid . . . . . .
> . . . ."

In vain have sorcerers kept telling me
That long and peaceful will my reign continue!...
But life and power fail to bring me joy:
I feel ill-luck and Heaven's wrath approaching.
I am unhappy. Haven't I sought to give
My people peace, prosperity and fame,
And win their love through generosity?!—
Alas! My hopes proved altogether vain:
The rabble hates the sight of living power;
They seem to love those only who are dead.
'Tis folly when, by popular applause
Or indignation wild, our hearts are shaken.
Almighty God has struck our land with famine;
The people started howling in distress;
And then to them all grain stores I threw open;
I gave them gold; I found for them employment:
And yet, they were the first to damn and curse
    me!
Their homes were razed by all-devouring fire,—
So I have promptly built for them new homes.
Yet, they accused me of committing arson!—
Such is the rabble's verdict, such their love!
Amongst my kin I looked for consolation:
A happy bride I meant to make my daughter,—
Like storm—alas!—death sweeps away her bride-
    groom...
Again, false rumors viciously are spread
That I am guilty, I, the ill-starred father!...
Whoever dies, I am the murderer:
I was the one who hastened Fëdor's death,
I was the one who poisoned the Czarina,
My humble sister-nun.... All crimes are mine!
I feel, there's nothing in this earthly life,
Amidst its grief, that gives us lasting peace;
Yes, naught... unless it be our conscience—

Clear conscience—that will always win and triumph
O'er wickedness, o'er dark and vicious slander;
Still, if it has but one, though slightest stain,
One single stain, that happens to besmirch it,—
Then all is lost: as in the flames of plague
The soul will burn, the heart be filled with poison;
Like hammers will reproaches smite the ears;
Disgust will rise, and turn the tortured head,
And bloodstained little boys will haunt and threaten,—
And one does long to flee, but whither? ... Dreadful!
Yea, wretched he whose conscience is not clear."

The shadow of the murdered child deprives Borís of the greatest treasure, his inner peace. Though dead, Dmitry lives in the Czar's afflicted conscience; nor can the menacing existence of a phantom be terminated by either poison or dagger. And so the bloodstained boy will become the lasting punishment for a grim and ghastly crime; he will assume his interrupted life in the guise of still another phantom—the False Dmitry, whose seemingly insane adventure will shake the rocks of a mighty Czardom.

Masterfully is Dmitry's nature revealed in Poushkin's play. The adventurous *parvenu* changes from one phase of his intricate personality to another: In Pimen's Cell, he is still a romantic dreamer; in the frontier Inn—an audacious bandit; in the Polish Castle—a shrewd impostor and suave diplomat; in the famous Fountain Scene —a passionately reckless lover, and we surmise that on the battle field he will prove a valiant soldier.

With all this, Dmitry is merely an episodic character: his ambitious plans of a bold pretender are cleverly used by Russia's enemies to their advantage. The fugitive monk clearly understands his rôle, and in the Fountain Scene, when speaking to Marína, he utters these challenging words:

> "Dost thou believe that I am fearing thee?—
> That trusted more will be a Polish maiden
> Than Russia's Princely Heir?—Still, thou shouldst know
> That neither King nor Pope nor any Noble
> Place faith in that which I am telling them.
> What do they care if I am really Dmitry?—
> I am a mere excuse for wars and strife,
> And this is all they care about."

Godounóv dies before False Dmitry has time to succeed in his plot. At the deathbed of the Czar, the boyars take an oath of allegiance to Fëdor, his adolescent son. But when the rebel forces triumph over the Moscow troops, the treacherous courtiers strangle their defenceless Sovereign. Again, this act of Destiny is but another way of handling the familiar "crime and punishment" theme. Ostensibly Borís dies reconciled with himself; still, the heavy hand of Fate strikes his beloved heir; with this death the Godounóv line comes to an end.

Though over a century old, *Borís Godounóv* today is just as fresh and immaculate as at the time when it was written; its characters are just as truthful and appealing; its dialogues and style—just as pure and perfect; its ideas—just as compelling and profoundly true. The critics' grumblings at minor flaws in the construction of the play are long forgotten, and Poushkin's great tragedy, outliving time, remains, as heretofore, one of the loftiest and most inspired creations of the human mind.

X

In the great, as in the little, the greatness of art may be revealed.

BORÍS GODOUNÓV has been warmly appreciated by the Russian public and was much treasured by Poushkin himself. Still, this tragedy was neither his concluding word, nor his greatest contribution to Russian dramaturgic repertory. After all, in *Borís Godounóv,* by the very nature of an historical drama, Poushkin was confined to specific situations and authentic characters; these, in a limited way only, permitted the treatment of such moral principles and psychological problems as might be called generic, primordial or inherent in human nature. Truly, history has its philosophy as philosophy has its history; yet, poetic works, designed to revive determined epochs, with their well-settled social backgrounds, necessarily circumscribe the scope and diapason of the artist's creative imagination by the element of historical reality or truth.

But the realism of Poushkin was broader than that approach to life which, for its expression, requires a chronological date or geographic localization. Nor were his taste for the dramatic and his passion for the unique limited to national tradition with its inevitable *couleur locale.* On the contrary, as Dostoievsky justly observed, Poushkin's nationalism did not atrophy his ingrained faculty—encountered in no other world artist—of reincarnating himself in the spirit, soul and living style of every other nation. His, then, was a realism of the universally real, which evades every barrier of space and every impediment of time.

For the interpretation of the immense, eternal and super-national, though unquestionably real, Poushkin devised a peculiar form of "Miniature Tragedies", which no one before—nor any one since—has dared to touch. In these brilliant sparkles of genius, one focal idea, one tragic antinomy between two fundamental laws or governing passions, is revealed with astounding economy of verbal material: the sentences are condensed to a point where it becomes impossible to omit from the text even a single line or seemingly casual word. Nor is it possible to change in any manner the syntactic construction of the phrases and their logical arrangement. Although, here, Poushkin preferably uses the five foot iambic blank verse, the meter remains unnoticed, or rather it conveys the impression of metric prose. This, indeed, is mathematics of literary thought. And then the psychological *crescendo* develops with such swiftness, impetus and sureness that one simply has no time to dwell upon anything else than the suddenly bursting storm of the crisis and its impending finale.

Poushkin's miniature theatre comprises four tragedies of this kind: *The Miser Knight, Mozart and Salieri, The Stone Guest,* and *The Feast During the Plague,* and, besides, the dramatic fragment *A Scene from Faust.* The first four plays were written by Poushkin in less than one month.

The Faust Scene—only a hundred and thirteen lines long—is a casual dialogue between the learned Doctor and his deceitful Leporello.

Faust is in a fatigued mood, and he says:

"I am weary, Demon.

Mephisto

Can't be helped!
Such is your everlasting fate
Which mortals never can surmount.
All creatures, which can contemplate,
Know boredom, be it on account
Of sloth and idleness, or whether
From over-work. One's faith is strong,

The other lost it altogether.
These are fed up with joy,—those long
For joy in vain. And yawningly
All live. And yawning waits for thee
The grave. So why shouldn'st thou yawn, too?"

Indeed, as Lao-Tze remarked: True words are not pleasant; pleasant words are not true, and Faust, the *homo sapiens,* knows that Mephisto has spoken the truth. Like a faithful mirror, the mocking ghost reflects Faust's own morbid tedium, that painful cleavage by which he is torn asunder: his mind, though filled with learning, is full of emptiness, and his "canon of reason" fatally assumes the form of an apotheosis of negation. This is the source of his weary loneliness and all-absorbing spleen. Still, the vital instinct compels him to cling to routine existence which, he knows, is hopelessly futile.

To Faust, the realm of learning is a world of boredom, and he exclaims:

"No life in knowledge, no delight:
I damned its false, seducing light."

But life in general has no solution to offer: even the sweet reminiscences about Gretchen are utterly ruined by Mephisto's cynical suggestion that, at the very moment when, in the silence of the night, the two palpitating hearts were ready to fuse in one chord of triumphant love, there was a third one present, a *tertius gaudens,* the evil genius himself, who cleverly instilled into the mind of Faust the poison of amorous illusions from which he later turns with horror and disgust.

The tragedy of ennui extends beyond this physical life of ours: even the obligingly gaping grave becomes the symbol of yawning Death.

In this vicious circle boredom reigns supreme, and solely because Faust's mind is weary and his soul craves for distraction of some kind, he orders the Demon to sink a schooner with a load of human lives.

In Russian literature, Poushkin's Faust gave birth to a long range of "needless beings" tormented by the incurable disease of modern skepsis, with its reflective reasoning, primordial weariness and undermining doubts. The pathological schism in Faust's consciousness, the sad sounds of his interminable elegy

*"Zwei Seelen wohnen—ach! in meiner Brust:—
Die eine will sich von der and'ren trennen"*

will be echoed and reëchoed by the successive generations of Russian Hamlets—by Lermontov's Pechórin, Turgenev's Rudin and Dostoievsky's Raskolnikov.

Perhaps even more pathetic than *Faust* is *The Miser Knight*—another magnificent creation of Poushkin's.

In this miniature play, composed of merely three fragmentary scenes, Poushkin depicts a sharp collision between two passions—avarice and dissipation. All his life the Baron, an old mediæval Knight, has been haunted by the sight of gold. Coin after coin, he has been adding to his hoard, and now the silent vaults under his stern castle conceal many a coffer filled with the precious gleaming metal. His is not a mere attraction to money, but a maniacal adoration, a religious cult, in which not the objectively real, but its imaginary reflection, acquires the guise of reality itself. He loves wealth not for its own sake, but because of its mystical and potential power. He meditates:

> "Indeed, what doesn't bow to me?—Like some
> Dark Demon, I, from hence, can rule the world:
> A whim—and stately mansions will arise,
> And lovely nymphs, in gayly smiling crowds,
> My gorgeous parks will suddenly invade;
> And Muses, too, will come and pay their tribute;
> And genius free to me will humbly bow;
> And virtue, and assiduous, sleepless labor
> Submissively will wait for my reward.
> A whistle is enough—and, timidly,
> Will bloodstained villainy creep up to me,
> Will lick my hands, will look into mine eyes,
> My will in them attempting to discern.
> Obedient is all to me, but I—
> To nothing. Yes, I soar above all wishes.
> I'm calm. I know my might, and this conviction
> Is all I need...."

The Baron has a son by the name of Albert, a careless youthful spendthrift, whose only concern

THE MIGHTY THREE

are women, feasts and tournaments. Albert is the Baron's *bête noire,* and a clash between the two cannot be avoided. The miser father divulges his hidden fears, while attending in silent solitude a strange feast, a sinister orgy of cupidity, which he has arranged for himself in the dark vaults of his castle:

"Today a feast I'm staging for myself:
A candle I shall light before each coffer,
And then I shall unlock them all, and shall
Be looking on at these gold glaring heaps.
    (Lights the candles and unlocks every coffer, one after the other).
I reign supreme! . . . What an enchanting
    glare! . . .
Obedient and mighty is my Kingdom!
In it—my honor, happiness and fame. . . .
I reign supreme! . . . And yet, who will succeed
    me
In my majestic heritage?—My heir?—
That spendthrift fool! . . . That youthful dissipator!
That faithful friend of rackish debauchees!—
As soon as I be dead, he will descend
To these pacific, dumb and silent vaults,
Amidst a crowd of flatt'ring greedy courtiers,
And stealing from my frigid corpse the keys,
With merry laughs, he will unlock the coffers,
And my belovèd treasures will begin
To flow through silken pockets full of holes!
He will destroy these sacred old containers!
He'll mix with dirt the Kingly holy oil!—
He'll dissipate!" . . . .

The peak of the miser's tragedy is reached with the words: *"He'll dissipate."*

In a conversation with the Duke, the Sovereign of the Land, the Baron falsely accuses Albert of an attempt to rob him. The son happens to overhear this calumny; he rushes in and calls his father a liar. And then, the old Knight, in a classically chivalresque fashion, throws his glove into Albert's face. The son catches it with the ironically gallant remark:

"Merci. This is my father's only gift."

The emotion caused by the violent dispute proves too great a strain on the old Baron; he collapses and dies exclaiming: "I'm choking! The keys! Where are my keys?"

Gogol's Plushkin in *The Dead Souls* is a wretchedly petty and untidy miser. Shylock and Harpagon are also utterly repulsive. But Poushkin masterfully avoids introducing into the treatment of the ugly sin—and avarice certainly is a sin—the element of the banal and mean. His miser is preëminently a *Knight,* and his vice is purified by passion—the trivial is purged in tragic atmosphere.

The same creative trait, but even stronger, appears in *Mozart and Salieri.* Here, too, the meanest of all vices—envy—is cast through the prism of the pitiful and personal drama of a studious, but wingless artisan, a sad specialist, who labors day and night in an endeavor to disclose the catechistic rules of counterpoint and the mysteries divine of harmony.

A stubborn ascetic of Art, Salieri finally succeeds in developing a "musical ear" and achieving "obedient but dry agility" in his fingers. He has won a reputation but not fame. In days long past, Salieri used to envy Haydn, but Haydn died. He now envies Mozart, on whom the heedless gods have abundantly bestowed two priceless gifts—a lucid talent and radiant inspiration. All by himself, incessantly brooding over the glory of Mozart's genius compared with his own dull and sterile skill, Salieri gradually conceives and silently nourishes the base intent of getting rid of Mozart:

"What use is there in him?—Like some pure
 cherub,
From Heaven a few chants he brought to us,
As if to wake in us, poor sons of dust,
A wingless hope, and then to wing away.
So do depart! The sooner, then, the better!"

Many a year ago, Salieri loved a woman: Izóra died bequeathing but one token of her love to him —a phial of deadly poison. All these years, he kept it hidden, just waiting for the moment when he could use it to "remove" a triumphant rival, whoever he might be. And Mozart did become his rival.

One day, happy as a sunbeam, Mozart burst into Salieri's house, and, rather casually, he started playing on the piano a musical creation of his own which, only the night before, he had composed. With the last sounds, turning to Salieri, he asked:

"How do you like this?

> *Salieri*
>
> What depth!
> What daring and what perfect harmony!
> Thou, Mozart, art a god, and yet, thou know'st
> This not: I know this, I."

And Mozart:

> "Oh really?! That may be!...
> But hungry is my deity."

Salieri hastens to invite his friend to dine with him at the Golden Lion Inn. Mozart accepts the invitation and leaves Salieri. Now, the caudal sting of envy pierces the wound of Salieri's heart. No longer can he resist his fate. At last, the poison of Izóra will serve its tragically useful end; it will silence Mozart's seraphic hymns:

> "The time has come!—Oh, sacred gift of love,
> Transfuse thyself into the cup of friendship!"

The concluding scene transpires in the Inn. Salieri commits the vile crime, and, already poisoned, Mozart plays his immortal *Requiem*. Sud-

THE MIGHTY THREE 147

denly, he begins to feel dazed and drowsy. He bids his friend goodbye. Like Poe's hero, Salieri could have whispered the ironic *"In pace requiescat"* farewell, for soon the Cherub, homeward bound, will have started winging back to Paradise.

By means of this terrestrial murder Salieri seeks to remedy an accidental error of Heaven—that vacuum of which Spinoza's geometrical God is the unchallenged Potentate. To Salieri's cold and calculating mind, supreme justice must be founded upon the principle of universal *order,* presupposing an *even* distribution of material and spiritual riches; but in the phenomenon of Mozart—and Salieri conceives in him, not a human being composed of blood and flesh, but merely an abstract phenomenon—the democratic law of equality has been offended and disturbed. Salieri's is a murder growing out of frigid dialectics. In this sense, he is the undying prototype of all rational murderers, and, undeniably, Poushkin's Salieri is the forefather of Dostoievsky's Smerdiakov.

In *Mozart and Salieri,* as in his other four miniatures, the tragedy develops with simplicity and inflexible vigor reminding one of the greatest creations of Sophocles or Shakespeare.

The linguistic properties of all these unequalled and unchallenged *chefs-d'œuvre* of world dramaturgy are absolutely flawless. Even if there were nothing more in Poushkin than these few hundred superbly chiselled and compressed lines, he might have been justly claiming his place among the immortals of all nations and all times.

XI

The skies are painted with unnumber'd sparks,
They all are fire and every one doth shine,
But there's but one in all doth hold his place . . .
    Julius Cæsar

                                    SHAKESPEARE

THE dramatic instinct of Poushkin, which inspired him to create *Borís Godounóv* and the whole group of miniature tragedies, found its final, most powerful and most perfect expression in *The Bronze Horseman,* a poem in rhyme and tetrametric iamb, dedicated to the Mighty Peter as he had been cast on the Falconet equestrian monument.

In *The Bronze Horseman,* Peter is shown in the process of a titanic struggle with three elements: The impersonal will of Nature; the passive, but elemental, resistance of obsolete Russia to his daring projects, and finally, the blind element of the vulgar majority revolting against the volcanic will of the Russian Cæsar.

First scene. Peter, statuesque and silent, stands on the marshy banks of the Neva, gazing into the misty distance. This is a picture of a great thought's birth: Peter decides to erect in the wilderness of the Northern forests, on the dreary Finnish swamps, a new capital for that State which is destined to become the greatest Empire in the Universe. His decision is dictated by considerations of sovereign importance: From hence, Russia will command the approaches to the sea; this will be her "window into Europe", and here will be laid the firm foundation of a new era—the Moscow *Czardom* shall yield to the Russian *Empire*.

Peter knows that, by undertaking this heroic action, he is challenging at once two elements: Nature, and Russia herself, dreadful in her motionless silence, inertly opposing his creative visions. But Peter is going to subdue both elements. Along his path he will smash all obstacles; he will transgress all barriers; he will crush all resistance. Peter will conquer.

Even in the Prologue the Great Monarch appears triumphant. He masters Nature which bows to his bold determination. Only one century later

"........ the youthful town,
Of Northern lands the graceful wonder,
Arose in splendor and renown
'Midst swamps and woods extending yonder.
Where, lonely, in the days long past,
The Finnish fisherman forlorn
In somber waters used to cast
His old worn fishnet ev'ry morn,—
Today—how diff'rent all looks there:
'Long lively shores rich mansions glare,
And stately buildings shine and tower;

> From lands remote and near, in pack,
> Ships glide along the river track,
> At harbors docking ev'ry hour;
> In granite Neva now is clad,
> Above her tides suspended bridges,
> While dark green gardens cover ridges
> Of islands yonder smiling glad."

The impossible has been achieved: the fogs of the Finnish swamps are now miraculously compressed into the granite of the lustrous city.

But Russia?—How does Peter conquer her?—Says Poushkin:

> "And 'fore the new born city now
> Old Moscow lost its ancient pride,
> As does the dow'ger Empress bow
> To the ascending Sov'reign's bride."

The second scene unfolds itself shortly thereafter. In 1824, upon the city of St. Peter a great catastrophe was wrought: The Neva overflowed her banks and inundated the capital. This calamity tore out of the mouth of Alexander the Blessed a despairing exclamation:

> ". . . . With *God's* grim elements
> The *Czars* are helpless to contend. . . ."

Still, amidst general consternation, one remains motionless, statuesque, unyielding.

That is Peter.

The terrible element of revolting Nature proves

powerless to shake the element of Peter's iron will. Around him—chaos of wildly roaring waves; fearful groans of a hurricane; and yonder—in the distance, panic-stricken, timidly cowering, stands Eugene, the so-called hero of the poem, one of those humble, lilliputian specimens of the human race whose name is—Legion. Majestic and grand, full of haughty disdain, Peter turns his back to him:

> "In heights above, unshaken, soaring
> Above the floods of Neva roaring,
> His hand extended with bold force,
> The giant sits on his bronze horse."

Peter remains motionless.

Such is his first encounter with the element of mediocrity.

Insistently, Poushkin emphasizes the colorless and impersonal character of Eugene. Even his family name is not mentioned; his are undetermined features of a person without a personality.

Like Gogol's hero in *The Cloak,* Eugene is only a microscopical screw, which shyly participates in the work of an enormous and soulless state machine. But what he is doing, how he is performing his routine functions,—we are not told.

Among the many tragedies caused by the inundation, there is one about which Poushkin tells a sad story: Eugene loves Parásha—a humble girl—living somewhere on the outskirts of the distressed city. After a stormy night, the Neva waters finally receded. Now Eugene speeds to his Parásha. But she is no more: She perished in the rioting floods, and even the wooden house in which she used to dwell, was washed away into the sea.

Eugene's is a personal drama; it is the grief of a weak creature dissolved in the incoherent grey multitude of a muzzled populace. The human is crushed by the weight of the superhuman.

As a unit, Eugene is impotent and not dangerous in the least. Yet, that same unit, multiplied by a countless quantity of similar units, is converted into something menacing, growing to the proportions of an element—the colossal aggregate of the human mass—the most treacherous of all elements.

One more scene. Some months later, the air of the capital was again breathing with storm. A gale was swelling up the turbulent and unruly waters of the Neva, and it was night. On his way home, Eugene was passing by the bronze monument of the Northern Titan:

> "Terrific stands he in the dark!
> And on his brow what thoughtful mark!
> What power looms in him and grows!
> And in that steed, what fiery force!
> Where art thou speeding, noble horse,
> And where shallst thou thine hoofs repose?—
> Oh, mighty Potentate of Fate!
> Didn'st thou, as with an iron rein,
> Jerk o'er a precipice in strain,
> Throw on her haunches Russia great?!"

Long did Eugene gaze at the mighty statue, and vividly came to his mind the sorrowful death of poor Parásha. Gradually, a feeling of revolt arose in his breast against him by whose despotic whim the capital was built. As if afflicted by some dark power, grinding his teeth, clenching his fist, he rancorously whispered: "All right, miraculous constructor!" ... This insane, but evil-wishing threat of a petty creature, suddenly makes the august cast of Peter quiver. Instantly, his face is lit by anger, and the hitherto motionless Sovereign begins a wild pursuit of the helpless slave. Eugene is overwhelmed with fear,

> "He runs, and hears behind his back,
> As though of thunder dreadful rumbles,
> Of heavy leaps incessant grumbles
> On pavement stones that shake and crack.—
> The moon illumes the giant Norseman,
> His hand extended with bold force,
> Pursues his chase the Iron Horseman
> On that loud clanging bounding horse."

From that nightmare, Eugene never recovers. Like Parásha, he falls a victim of the Great Peter.

Strange seems this unequal struggle between the Bronze Giant and a paltry clerk, who later will transform himself into Gogol's Akáki Akákievich, Turgenev's Koúzvokin, Chekhov's Váflia, into a dull anthropoid vegetating in interminable multiplications throughout the vast and endless spaces of the proud Empire. But Poushkin prophetically foresaw that precisely the impersonal human mass, the element of the Little, will become the most dreadful and hardly escapable threat to the Great, of which the Bronze Horseman is the immortal Symbol.

XII

L'enfance passe, mais l'enfantillage reste.

STILL as a young man, burning with passion and untempered longings, Poushkin arrived in Mikháilovskoie. He left the place of his exile with a mind fully matured and his creative "I" brought in accord with the world around him. By this time he had reached perfection in his poetic work, giving full exhibition of his mighty genius.

Baudelaire remarked once that Delacroix, the famous French animalist, "was passionately in love with passion, and coldly determined to seek the means of expressing passion in the most graphic form." Such had also become Poushkin as a result of his long seclusion and uninterrupted mental growth. Master, indeed, of form, he learned the secret of unmistakably balancing the outward mode of artistic workmanship with the inner substance of his creative dreams. Poushkin, as poet, had reached the state of final equilibrium.

The purely poetical phase of his work came to a climax, attaining that level of excellency which no Russian poet has since exceeded. Today, the wreath of Poushkin's rhymes lies in the marble Pantheon of Fame, as ever, fresh, unfading, amaranthine.

In words full of enthusiasm and praise, Bielinsky summarized the signal qualities of Poushkin's poetry:

> "Poushkin's verse"—he said—"in its original creations, made, as it were, a sharp turn, a definite departure from the prior history of Russian poetry, breaking with its traditional forms and revealing something hitherto unknown ... And what a verse it is! Antique plasticism and classical simplicity blend in perfect harmony with the alluring melodies of the romantic rhyme. The entire acoustic wealth, the full might of the Russian tongue, are expressed here with astounding completeness: now it is tender, sweet and soft, like murmurs of the waves; now it is ductile and pliant as wax; flaring like lightning; pure and transparent as crystal; fragrant as the breath of Spring; hard and vigorous like the blows of a glaive in the hands of a Knight."

Temperamentally, however, Poushkin had never really settled down. Quoting Chénier he said about himself: *"Tel j'étais autrefois, et tel je suis encore."* Here is his confession:

> "Such as I used to be before, such am I still:
> So careless, amorous. You know, my friends, what thrill
> The beautiful evokes in my imagination!

> What timid tenderness, what hidden animation!
> Hasn't Love bestowed on me much worry and much plight?
> And haven't I been struggling, like a fledgling kite,
> In the seductive nets which Cypris threw around me?—
> And yet, despite the many thorns with which life crowned me,
> Alas! I still am worshipping new idols."

Released from his estate, he dashed back to St. Petersburg and Moscow, and there, once more, he was drawn into the vortex of social turmoil. Some of his lyrical verses of that period are strikingly suggestive of his blazing moods and unabated passion for Cypris, the Goddess of Passion. For a while, he was in love with Countess Zakrevsky, a beautiful, though somewhat amoral woman, whom he himself so graphically described:

> "By stormy passion driven forth,
> And with her sultry soul all glaring,
> Amongst ye, matrons of the North,
> She reappears at times. With daring,
> She disregards all world's relations:
> A lawless comet, in her course,
> She speeds along with reckless force,
> Amidst well settled constellations."

And, of course, besides the Countess, there were other women—some more, others less, responsive —but each one, in her own whimsical way, most captivating and charming: Catherine Timásheva, for instance, or Oushakóva, or Olénina, to whom he penned this musing wee-bit on her fair self and her occasional swoops upon the Northern Capital:

"Pompous city! City lean!
Servile spirit! Stately glare!
Skies above—in pallid green.
Boredom. Granite. Chilly air!
Yet, on guard I should be put,
For in our urban whirl
Treads, at times, a little foot,
And there weaves a golden curl."

But to one of the less responsive of his inamoratas the poet dedicated *The Nightingale,* a half elegiac little poem:

"In Spring, when silent parks are covered by the veil
Of night,—in vain sings to the rose the eastern nightingale:
The rose does not respond, and through the slumb'ring hours,
The hymns of love fail to awake the queen of flowers.
Thus also are thy songs, oh poet, sung in vain:
In frigid beauty they evoke no joy, no pain;
Her bloom thrills thee; thy heart is filled with admiration,
And yet, her heart stays cold, and void of animation."

So Poushkin lived through the last years of his free bachelor life, as it were, in an endless amorous rondo.

However, the latter part of the Twenties' marked a new tendency in Poushkin's literary evolution: Slowly he started deviating from pure lyricism, paying ever-increasing attention to popular themes, prose and historical research. In the early Thirties', in addition to his miniature tragedies, he wrote several folk tales, among which three—*The Tale About Czar Saltán, The Tale About the Fisherman and the Fish* and *Coq d'Or* —are very properly regarded as creations unsurpassed in naïve sincerity and poetic style.

XIII

*Tales are dreams, and yet they tend
To promote some useful end.*
                                        POUSHKIN

FOR some reason, Russian writers, with the exception of Dostoievsky and a few others, have paid little attention to the place which popular legends and folk tales occupy in the literary heritage of Poushkin, even though this particular group of his creations is extremely characteristic of our poet's cardinal trait—his faithful nationalism, of which Arína Rodiónovna was the half conscious beginning and the *Coq d'Or* the brilliant conclusion.

Poushkin had an instinctive love for that which is being reverently carried and lastingly fondled in

THE MIGHTY THREE

the bosom of a people's consciousness, becoming blood of the blood and flesh of the flesh of national life. And there was nothing more popular—in Russia, at least,—than her folk tales and folk songs. From the dawn of history, the human mind has always been profoundly influenced by the rhythmic properties of Nature. Through centuries and ages, man has been intuitively striving to adapt himself to that mysterious Force which moulds the universal order, and preordains the destinies of that which is and was and ever will be—a Force at once the cause and symbol of harmony itself. Of this subconscious, but ardent, yearning for rhythm and beauty, the song and tale are the most radiant expressions.

At times, it is not easy to draw a line between the fading murmurs of long forgotten legends and the dark beginnings of what purports to be history.

Like every other Wonderland, the Russian fairy world came into being through slow formation of successive layers recording the incessant changes in the beliefs, psychology, morality, official cults and occult visions of the Russian people. In Poushkin's own words:

"That's Russia! That is Russian spirit!"

Ingenuous as it be, the folk tale is never a mere bagatelle; always there is some ancient story behind it, some moral expressive of a somberly suspected, though living truth. With full justification, then, Poushkin concluded his *Coq d'Or* with the saying that

> "Tales are dreams, and yet they tend
> To promote some useful end."

This is particularly so in the case of the story about the Fisherman and the Fish: the popular mind condemns greed and vanity as vices, of which the Fisherman's wife is a vivid emblem. The opening lines of the Tale are pervaded with a calm and epic atmosphere:

> "Once there lived an old man and old woman
> On the shore of a sea, blue and deep;
> There they lived in a humble old mud-hut,
> Fully thirty and three lonely years.
> The old man was engaged in his fishing,
> The old woman—in spinning her yarn.
> Once the man threw his net in the water,—
> Naught but seaweed the net did bring back;
> Then again he submergèd his fishnet,—
> Still with nothing but grass it came up.
> So he dipped his worn net for the third time,—
> And a gold fish was caught in the net,—
> Not a plain fish—the net brought a gold fish!
> And the little gold fish started praying,
> In a human voice making her plea:
> 'Throw me back in the sea, dear old fisher!
> For my freedom I'll pay a high price:
> I shall give thee whatever thou wishest!'
> The old man was astonished and frightened:
> Three and thirty long years he'd been fishing,

But had never heard sea-folk use speech.
So he threw the gold fish in the water,
With these words full of kindly intent:—
'May God bless thee, my dear little gold fish!
Me don't want to accept thy reward;
Do swim freely about in the water,
Do return to the sea, blue and deep.'

The old man then returned to his woman,
And about the great wonder he told her:
'Me today almost caught quite a fish!
Not a plain fish—my net brought a gold fish!
In our own human tongue she was speaking,
And she begged me to let her go home;
A high price did she offer for freedom,
Granting me any gift I might wish.
But me dared not to take any ransom;
So me let her return to the sea.'
The old woman then started to scold him:—
'Oh, ye fool! Silly goose-cap, thou art!
Not to take a reward from the fish!—
For a trough thou, at least, should have asked;
Look, our own has all fallen apart.' "

The old man then returned to the sea, and he called for the gold fish, telling her about his woman's desire:

"And thus spake the wee-fish to the fisher:
'Do not worry, old man! May God bless thee!—
Ye shall have the new trough that ye wish'th.' "

But *l'appetit vient en mangeant,* and the woman first insists on having a new cottage, then she is pictured as a social climber, and she says:

"Me don't want to be merely a peasant,
But a lady of noble degree."

This honor, when granted by the wonder fish, does not appease her ambition, and she sends her husband back to the sea, demanding that the fish make her Queen of the Land. Even to this plea, the gold fish accedes, and the woman is crowned Queen. Now she dwells in a sumptuous palace, surrounded by a brilliant guard. But boundless is the craze of the woman's vanity: she gives this order to her humble old husband:

" 'Do return to the fish, and salute her!
Me don't want to be merely a Queen!
But me wishes to rule over oceans,
And to dwell in the sea, blue and deep,
With the fish, my obedient servant,
To fulfill ev'ry one of my whims.'

"The old man did not dare to oppose her;
Not a word did he dare to respond.
So once more he went back to the blue sea:
A black tempest was raging in fury;
Angry waves in huge swells, wildly leaping,
Rolled in thunder and roarèd and groaned.
He began to call out for the gold fish,
So she answered his call, and she asked:
'Tell me what dost thou wish, dear old fisher?'
Thus responded the man with a bow:
'Me applies to thy mercy, wee queen fish!
What to do with that cursèd old woman!—
She no longer is pleased to be Queen,—
Over oceans she wants to rule now,

And she wishes to dwell in the waters,
With thyself, her obedient servant,
To fulfill ev'ry one of her whims.'
No response gave the fish to the fisher;
With her tail she but splashèd the water,
Off she went to the depths of the sea.
The old man waited long for an answer,
But in vain. Back he went to his woman.
Lo! What's that?—He beholds his old mud-hut;
At the threshold his woman is sitting,
And before her—the broken, old trough."

In the two other folk tales (*Coq d'Or* and *Czar Saltán*), Poushkin once more reverts to the half legendary motives which, in his youthful days, he had used in moulding *Ruslán and Ludmíla*. Permeated with incomparable humor, these precious creations of a mirthful genius may be conceived as a canon of the pure, colorful and free Russian popular speech, notwithstanding the fact that these tales are rhymed. Here Poushkin conquered the seemingly insurmountable difficulties of the syntax and the most intricate riddles of poetic meter. The superb narrative flows in these folk tales as easily and naturally as in his lyrical pieces—those songs, now glad and happy, now sad and mournful, of his palpitating heart.

The *Coq d'Or* requires no protracted exegetic comment. Everybody knows the story of Czar Dadón, whose Kingdom gay is guarded by the Golden Cock. And it will be probably recalled that the fairy bird was given to Dadón by a "eunuch and sky-reader." Summoned by the Czar, the sage appears before him, and we will let Poushkin tell his own story:

> "In his bag he has in stock,—
> Only think!—a golden cock!
> 'To achieve', he said, 'thy goal,
> Place the bird on some high pole,
> And my golden cock will be
> Thy true guard o'er land and sea.
>
> 'Now, if peace and quiet reign,—
> Silent will the bird remain;
> But in case, from land or sea,
> War again should threaten thee,
> Or invasion should impend,
> Or ill-fate distress should send,—
> Instantly, to warn thine home,
> Will the gold cock raise his comb,
> Shake his wings and loudly crow,
> Turning t'wards the threat'ning foe.'
>
> "Czar Dadón, with joy untold,
> Pledged the wizard heaps of gold.
> 'For such service, which I treasure,'
> Czar Dadón exclaimed with pleasure,
> 'Thy first wish, as mine own will,
> I shall readily fulfill.' "

The little Cock faithfully discharges his duties:

> "Slight as may the danger seem,
> The true guard, as in a dream,
> Starts to move and shake his wings
> Towards the side that danger brings,
> And 'Kiri-koo-koó', he crows,
> 'Reign and peacefully repose!' "

But the Czar breaks his pledge when the eunuch comes to claim his reward: He refuses to surrender the beautiful Circassian Queen with whom, in the interim, he had fervently fallen in love. In a fit of anger Czar Dadón strikes the sky-reader on his head, and then comes the expiation scene, where the Cock avenges his dead master:

"He flies straightway to the car,
On the bald head of the Czar
He alights; he shakes his wings;
Pecks Dadón, and off he swings.
Czar Dadón fell down and sighed,
Gasped his last—and thus he died.
No one since that day has seen,
The Circassian fairy Queen."

By its freshness and sparkling youth, Poushkin's Tale has captured the imagination of the busy Western World; it has been translated by Rimsky-Korsakoff into a grand poem of enchanting sounds, while the Golden Cock, after having fulfilled the mission of wrathful, but just Fate—after having pecked Czar Dadón's bald head—has once more alighted on the high mast of Poushkin's fame.

Though less known, yet not less charming, is *The Tale About Czar Saltán,* which also inspired Rimsky to write an opera of the same name.

Like a piece of precious *point de Maligne,* the story is a classical and composite delineation of folk themes, borrowed from the chattering legends of the Russian fairy world. In an endless row, adventure after adventure unfolds itself in pictures full of ardor and joy. When reading *Czar Saltán,* one has the sensation of attending a splendid feast, where all is magic and wonder and color and sound—a glorious galaxy of animation, luster and shine.

The introductory scene is quite in line with the general tone, mirthful and light, of Poushkin's story:

> "Three fair sisters, young and bright,
> Near their window spun, one night;
> One maid said:—'I truly mean,
> If I only were a Queen,
> For the people, dear and strange,
> Gorgeous feasts I would arrange.'
> 'And if I Queen could be made,'
> Said the second charming maid,
> 'For the whole world, I believe,
> Linen I would gladly weave.'
> 'If a crown 'fore me be laid,'
> Thus remarked the third young maid,
> 'For the Czar, with love and care,
> I would bear a knightly heir.'
> As she spake—and nothing more—
> Gently creaked the wooden door,
> And the Czar, from out the gloom,
> Stepped into the maidens' room.
> He had heard the last girl's pledge,
> Standing hid behind the hedge.
> Mighty glad he was to share
> Girlish dreams about an heir.
> 'Gentle maiden, young and bright,
> Be a Queen and bear a knight!—

> To the heir, thou must remember,
> I look forward in September.
> As to you, my sisters dear,'
> Said the Czar, 'you need not fear!—
> Leave your home, and follow me
> And your sister cheerfully:
> *Thou* a weaver deft shall be,
> And a cook I'll make of *thee*.' "

A rich feast is given in celebration of Czar Saltán's wedding, and Poushkin confidentially informs us:

> "That same night, in ardor keen,
> As she promised, the young Queen
> Started to beget an heir."

Sadly, the brave Czar was soon forced to leave his young bride: a war broke out and, *volens-nolens*, he had to defend his Kingdom against the invading enemy. It must have been a protracted fight, since in September he was still far away from home, while, without waiting for his return, the Queen bore a sturdy son. This happy event, however, proved the beginning of many a misfortune. The envious sisters hastened to send to the King this libelous message:

> "Thy Queen bore, as though for fun,
> Neither daughter, neither son,
> Neither frog, nor mouse in feature,
> But a strange and awkward creature."

A few days later, the wicked maids produced a forged decree from the grieved Czar ordering that the Queen and her newborn be sealed in a barrel and tossed into the sea. Then comes this picture:

> "In the blue sky stars are flashing;
> In the blue sea waves are splashing;
> In the dark sky clouds are shifting;
> In the sea a cask is drifting.
> In the cask the Queen is weeping;
> In her arms the child is sleeping.
> And the boy, in brawn and power
> Gains and grows, from hour to hour.
> Days go by. The Queen's despair
> Is no less. But her young heir
> Speeds the waves:—'Oh, restless wave!
> Thou art free and thou art brave!
> Splashest thou in mighty play,
> Gloomy rocks thou wear'st away,
> Strands thou overflow'st with roar,
> And thou drivest ships ashore!
> Do not wreak on us thy hate!
> Land us safely! Save our fate!'
> And the wave obeyed this plea:
> So the cask, from out the sea,
> She tossed gently on the strand,
> And receded from the sand."

Now mother and son are safe on a fairy island. All sorts of wonders transpire there, while Gvidón, Saltán's son, becomes the happy ruler over that remote realm. Serene as his life is, he is sadly missing his father. Fate, in the guise of a beautiful Lady-Swan, favors the reunion of the family. Rumors about the Island of Bouyan have reached the Czar, and his interest is aroused by its variegated attractions. Among these, not the least is a darling little squirrel, busily engaged in an occupation which Poushkin describes so:

> "Once more filled with hope and joy,
> Homeward goes the happy boy.
> As he steps into his yard,
> Lo!—a pine tree, keeping guard,
> Upright stands, and 'round folks gazing
> At a squirrel. It's amazing:—
> She cracks gold nuts; in her claws—
> Em'rald kernels; little paws
> File the shells in even heaps.
> With a gentle whiz, she keeps
> Softly singing this sweet air:—
> 'In the garden, maiden fair!'"

At last, the cherished day comes when Czar Saltán, escorted by a brilliant retinue, including the weaver and the cook, lands at the capital of Prince Gvidón. He is dazzled by the sight of its smiling gardens and golden domes. Now all wonders unroll before his eyes. A happy reunion this really was! And the Czar, overwhelmed by benevolence, promptly granted full amnesty to the weaver and the cook.

The tale would not have ended right without a sumptuous feast, after which

> "Czar Saltán, in ravings sunk,
> Fell asleep that night, half-drunk."

Poushkin adds that he happened to have been present at the revelry and that

> "Mead and beer he drank and yet,
> Naught but whiskers did he wet."

Such is *der langen Rede kurzer Sinn*.

XIV

La grammaire qui sait régenter jusqu'aux rois.

POUSHKIN, the Shakespeare of Russian poesy, must also be conceived as the Walter Scott of Russian prose; he conveyed to its grammatical build —classically simple as a Bach fugue—mathematical precision. He was the first to grasp the now generally acknowledged fact that prose, in order to be impressive, must follow certain well defined architectonic laws, which convey to the outline of the written word a musical flow or metrical touch. Accordingly, his are laconic, divided, as it were, in octosyllabic cola, and perfectly carved sentences, like those of which the Miniature Tragedies are composed.

In Poushkin's prose, the rule of verbal economy has been followed with unfailing, perhaps even rigid, logic. His style is a direct negation of rhetoric verbosity—not one superfluous word, not a single unwarranted punctuation mark: clear thoughts expressed in well-balanced and precise words. This standard of prose reminds one of a Doric column, that unfading symbol of simplicity and beauty.

THE MIGHTY THREE 171

Novelettes such as *The Undertaker, The Storm* and *The Shot,* unsurpassed in workmanship, have become models for that kind of fiction which is now known as *short stories.*

Applying to prose the principles of his own poetry, Poushkin achieved the maximum imaginative effect by the use of a minimum number of words. Take this passage from the poem *Poltava:*

> "All calm is the Ukrain'an night.
> The sky is clear. The stars shine bright.
> The air, in drowsy meditation,
> Is dormant. Gentle palpitation
> In poplar leaves evokes a sound.
> On White-Church, from its tranquil height,
> The moon sheds beams of fairy light,
> Illumining the gorg'ous park
> And Hetman's castle, stern and dark.
> And calm is everything around."

In a metrical text such as this, the demarcation line between poetry and prose seems to be altogether effaced: poetry merges with prose; prose assumes the guise of poetry. The construction of phrases is impossible of either improvement or change.

Such is, not the style, but the living canon, of the Poushkin prose; such we find it not only in his short stories, but equally in his longer novels: *The Captain's Daughter, Doubróvsky, The Egyptian Nights,* and *The Queen of Spades.* Each one of these stories is not only equal to, but, in sincerity of expression and purity of form, exceeds Lermontov's *The Hero of Our Times* or Tolstoy's *The Cossacks,* superb creations though these are.

Another excellent work in prose is Poushkin's *History of the Pougachév Rebellion,* which, in addition, is a brilliant historical account of a rather involved and obscure uprising of the Ural Cossacks which took place in the Eighteenth Century during the reign of Catherine the Great.

The impetuosity of the narrative, the chastity of the language, and what Mirsky calls, the "compact terseness" of the grammar in these exhibits of Russian literary taste and style, have hardly anything comparable in world literature.

By this time, the genius of Poushkin had fully blossomed out. His spirit soared to ever loftier planes of artistic achievement. From these heights, infinite distances revealed themselves to our poet's vision, and today, who will venture to suggest how far and how deep his inspired thought would have reached if fate had not mercilessly interrupted the majestic flow of his creative meditations?

XV

So gleams the past, the light of other days. . . .
BYRON

WHICH one of the great works of Poushkin should be considered the greatest?—This is largely a matter of opinion, since in our poet's artistic heritage there are so many perfect creations that it is, indeed, difficult to select among them any particular one in preference to others, equally ingenious and beautiful. Here we have to contend with a typical case of *embarras de choix*.

Still, it is undeniable that in *Eugene Onegin,* Poushkin has expressed himself more freely and more exhaustively than in any other of his major poems.

"*Onegin*"—says Bielinsky—"is Poushkin's most intimate creation, the most beloved child of his fantasy, and there are but few works in which a poet's personality would be drawn out with such a completeness, so serenely and lucidly, as Poushkin's ego has been reflected in *Onegin*. Here is his whole life, his soul, his love; here—his sentiments, conceptions and ideals."

But *Eugene Onegin* is not a mere autobiographical account or an author's confession about the things he had dreamed in the days when he was young. In this work, Poushkin carved the characters out of the very flesh of Russian life, which he depicted so truthfully that he who wishes to comprehend Russia's past must begin with the study of *Eugene Onegin*. Here, we find unfolded a multi-colored picture of Russia's town and country, with a mass of living detail which, like sweet-scented flowers, are freely strewn all over the vast grounds of a virtuosic narrative outliving the wear and tear of fading time.

Like one of those Bartalozzi mezzotints, the general tone of this famous novel is graceful, humorous and light, here and there, touched in gold of the rising sun's first smiling beams, or tipped with silver of sighing sorrow—illusions and disillusions fused together, just as in everybody's experience, and just as smiles and sorrows were part of Poushkin's own life. For there is, in this work, a great deal of autobiographical material which the poet does not bashfully conceal from his audience even when he happens to reveal some trait of his intrinsic deviltry. Take these lines:

> "By Fate Eugene was safely guided:
> To *Mádame* first he was confided,
> And then *Monsieur* took care of him.
> The child was sweet, but full of whim.
> *Monsieur l'Abbé,* a humble Frenchman,
> In order not to tire the child,
> Instructed him in manner mild,
> Becoming his indulgent henchman.
> . . . .
> But when, in line with nature's fashion,
> Upon Eugene youth cast her grace—
> The age of hopes and tender passion—
> *Monsieur* was told to quit his place."

This certainly is suggestive of Poushkin's own childhood.

In the history of Russia's intellectual development, *Eugene Onegin* became a landmark of major moment. As Professor Kluchevsky said:

> "This was an event of our youth; a biographical trait of ours; a break in our growth similar to that which is occasioned by college graduation or the first love."

Poushkin devoted at least eight years of his life to the moulding and remoulding of *Eugene Onegin,* which is a novel of eight chapters in verse and rhyme. In the days when the work was originally conceived, Poushkin was still living through his Byronic period, and Byron's impress upon the character of Eugene is quite obvious. But here, again, Poushkin succeeded in preserving his independence of an artist, and the complex type of Onegin himself comprises many psychological ingredients and historical antecedents, all of which stand in no relation to the Byronic philosophy.

Nor was Poushkin at all sure as to which anthropological class his hero really belonged. Half-seriously he asked these questions:

> "What is he then?—An imitation?
> A worthless phantom?—Or perhaps,
> Just one of Moscow's many chaps
> In Harold's guise?—Or a translation
> Of other people's whims and moods?"
> . . . .

No doubt, Childe Harold's mantle was an important feature in Onegin's attire. But there is a long genealogical history behind Onegin—a past evolution which dates back to the early part of the Eighteenth Century: the fathers of the Russian Onegins began their studies under Elizabeth; they completed their education under Catherine, and leisurely slumbered through their senescence under Alexander. This genetic background constitutes a peculiar mixture of Peter's stern traditions, Voltaire's skepticism, the grand covenants of Racine, and the petty vices of a wealthy aristocracy which bred on *dolce far niente* and was nourished by gaunt serfdom.

Nor is there any question that in his descending lineage Onegin was the forefather of a whole company of wanton heroes, such as Lermontov's Pechórin, Goncharóv's Raisky, Turgenev's Roudin and Lavretzky, Dostoievsky's Raskolnikov, and so many others. In this or that sense, in one measure or another, they are all afflicted with a marked inferiority complex, which has been fitly stated in the well-known sentence:

> "We are born for daring impulses,
> But achievement—is not our realm."

Polished and smart, but superficial and carefree, Onegin is a legitimate son of Russian nobility as it used to be in those remote days. A child "of luxury and play", the "eighteen year old philosopher" began to burn the candle of his life at an age when he should have been diligently attending school, and he grew fatigued even before he had done anything to be tired of.

The scope of Onegin's education was neither too extensive nor too profound. But he did, from his early youth, master "the science of tender passion", and all the subtle little tricks of deceiving and intriguing the fair sex, now by passionate declarations, and now, by pensively eloquent silence. A habitué of the ballet, Eugene grew fond of that half-veiled life "behind the scenes", those theatrical *dessous,* which are artfully concealed from the eyes of the uninitiated.

The radical commentators of the Sixties' accused Poushkin of having almost glorified in Onegin the model of a socially useless creature. But they seem to have overlooked the fact that Poushkin himself, when portraying his hero, entertained no illusions concerning the actual meaning of his moral character. Obviously, it was for this reason that he selected as an epigraph to the opening chapter of the novel this citation from a private letter:

> "Absorbed by vanity, he also possessed that kind of arrogance which made him view with equal indifference the bad things as well as the good—an attitude which was due to a feeling of superiority, imaginary perhaps."

Poushkin clearly understood that, by introducing Onegin to his readers, he was giving a vivid picture of those idle strata of Russian, or if you please, European society, whose existence was an incarnation of nothingness, and whose would-be disappointments—or to use the then fashionable term—whose "spleen", was the natural outgrowth of incurable indolence and lack of mental culture. Onegin's main trouble is that he has no aim in life, and he drifts along from day to day, according to Ruskin, "without fear, without pleasure, without horror, and without pity."

This vacuity of the spirit prompts him to give vent to hopeless lamentations:

> "Oh why, like Tula's poor taxator,
> Am I not lying paralyzed?
> Why am I not, at least, chastised
> By rheumatism?! . . . Oh Creator!
> . . . .
> The ill are happy: They can figure
> That o'er them hangs Fate's heavy glaive,
> But I am young and full of vigor!
> I'm bored, and craving for the grave!"

Fate interrupts the monotonous diversity of Onegin's social adventures on the Neva banks, and chance transplants him to his estate where he begins to dwell in dull seclusion. But soon he meets Lensky, a young poet, an admirer of Schiller and an adept of Goettingen's devious ideals. Between the two a friendship develops and, for a while, both seem pleased with each other.

Through Lensky, and on his insistence, Onegin makes the acquaintance of the Larins, an old-fashioned, simple, but hospitable family, in whose bosom there grow two lovely field flowers, two fair sisters—Olga and Tatiana.

Of Olga Poushkin gives this picture:

> "She, ever modest, bashful seeming,
> And always bright as sun at morn;
> As naïve as a poet's dreaming,
> And sweet, as when love's kiss is born;
> Her eyes as deep as heaven's blue;
> Her smiles, her locks of golden hue;
> Her maiden stature, voice and glance,—
> All that is Olga:—Choose by chance
> Some novel cheap, her portrait's there;
> 'Tis very pleasing; I admit
> I once was quite in love with it.
> But now its sight I cannot bear."

But Lensky *is* in love with Olga. They are even engaged, and soon the link of two loving hearts will be made stronger—who knows?—by the nuptial tie. Though charming, Olga is a *terre à terre* creature. Her feelings are shallow, light her moods, and, inconsequentially, she flits about like an iridescent butterfly.

How different Tatiana!—Timid as a doe in dreamy woods, she has never taken any fancy to the vivacious games of her youthful companions. She prefers pensive solitude, and even within the fold of her own family she seems a stranger.

> "But pensiveness, her true attendant,
> From tender days of cradle age,

> In hours of leisure, bright and splendent,
> Dream feasts for her did often stage."

Always meditating over something, always sorrowful and wistful, Poushkin tells us about Tatiana that

> ". . . her tender little fingers
> Despise the needle, as she lingers
> O'er silken patterns all aflame,
> And drowsy linen on the frame."

Since childhood, Tatiana has had an almost mystical adoration of Nature. Fond of her silent park and the golden fields around,

> "She loved to watch the morn's slow wading,
> Awaiting dawn's first smiling glance,
> When from the sky line, pale and fading,
> Stars disappear in choral dance."

As she grew older, Tatiana, just as Poushkin himself, contracted the delightful but somewhat dangerous habit of reading—a tendency which, in her case, could be hardly conceived as congenital, since

> "She always had a strong addiction
> To reading novels, soft and stern,
> She was in love with dreams, with fiction,
> Rousseau and Richardson, in turn;
> Her father, not a social climber,
> Was just a simple good old-timer,
> And while in books he saw no wrong,—
> For reading his distaste was strong."

Then comes the romance, an immortal *page d'amour* of a maiden's heart.

"*Elle était fille, elle était amoureuse.*"—Desperately Tatiana falls in love with Onegin, and after much fear and hesitation, she writes him a letter full of sentimental emotion. She knows that she is breaking all conventions, and she even starts her confession with a pathetic self-indictment:

> "I write to you! Is more required?
> Can lower depths beyond remain?—
> 'Tis in your power, if desired,
> To crush me with a just disdain." *

Alas! Her love evokes no echo in Onegin's sophisticated heart, and in a chilly sermon, he tells her:

> "I love you with a love of brother,
> Still stronger is my love, maybe."

He confesses that "he is not created for beatitude", nor adapted to the delights of domesticity. He wants to be free, and freedom—he argues—is incompatible with nuptial shackles.

Heartbroken, Tatiana listens to Onegin's lesson. She firmly knows that, having once given her heart to Onegin, she will never love again:

---
* These lines are quoted from Lieutenant Colonel Spalding's translation of Tatiana's letter.

> "*Das giebt's nur einmal!*
> *Das kommt nicht wieder....*"

Deep is her wound, and it will never quite heal. For Tatiana's heart is not governed by fleeting caprice or transient whims. Tatiana is a Russian woman whose heart, though soft and yielding, is firm and faithful; to her, self-sacrifice is not a pose or mood, but rather an irresistible response to love and duty. Tatiana is that captivating symbol of Russian womanhood which found its further interpretation in other dear images—in Turgenev's Lisa, Tolstoy's Natásha, Goncharóv's Vera, and Dostoievsky's Sonya. They all are victims of love, and of what they conceive to be their duty. Theirs is proud and concentric suffering; theirs is pain caused by eccentric circumstances, desecrating the "holy of holies" of their loyal hearts.

Onegin's and Tatiana's paths seem to be parting forever: *He* leaves her—still "absorbed by vanity", still wearing Childe Harold's moody mantle, with a mind perhaps more arid than ever, after his duel with Lensky, whom he so cruelly insulted and so wantonly killed; *She* is left by him—with a bleeding, but loving heart, determined to forget, ready to forgive, with a firm resolve to fulfill her duty, trying though it be.

In the ever-flowing tides of Time, as Heraclitus used to call it—"in the ceaseless flux of changes"—events appear and disappear, but life rolls its waves just the same.

THE MIGHTY THREE 183

A few years after Onegin's departure, Tatiana, acceding to the entreaties of her family, marries a brilliant General of high standing. Now, admitted to the Imperial Court, Tatiana shines as the brightest star in the aristocratic constellation of the Northern capital. And it so happens that Onegin, who, for years, has heard nothing about her who chose him for the hero of her dreams, returns to St. Petersburg after having wandered long and uselessly throughout Russia. Again, he is attracted by the luster and shine of social life; again, he divides his time between one ball and the next, while, *entre poire et fromage,* again, he feels ready to resume his amorous career.

Yet, Fate rules differently: At one of the social affairs, he sees a woman: She is "all harmony, all wonder." Surrounded by an admiring crowd and flattered by those who themselves are used to nothing but flattery, she displays her grace with divine indifference and calm. Onegin is thrilled, and he learns that this is Tatiana. Now he begins to worship her, whom in days past, he had treated as a *quantité négligeable.* Now he is in love, but

> "Not with that girl so shy and bashful,
> So poor, and simple, and in love,
> But with a princess unaffected,
> A goddess, perfect and selected,
> Of the majestic Neva shores."

Onegin's passion for Tatiana leaps and bounds. But she remains indifferent, cold and deaf. He writes her letter after letter, tender, flaming, apologetic. He confesses:

> "Once having met you, by mere fortune,
> Your love I marked. To my misfortune,
> Take heed of it I did not dare.
> That feeling then I have arrested;
> My freedom, worthless and detested,
> To lose, alas! I did not care."

His letters are ignored. The tortures of unreturned love grow so acute that he retires from society, and lives in solitude through the slow-creeping Winter. He fears he is going mad, but Poushkin, with his usual sense of humor, remarks that

> "... how it happ'd he did not know it:
> Long winter months began to wane,
> Yet he did not become a poet,
> Nor did he die nor grow insane."

Now Onegin makes his last effort to win Tatiana's affection: Once more he sees her, and kneeling before her, he eloquently tells her of his love and sufferings and dreadful regrets about the fatal error which, years ago, when he first met her, he had so carelessly committed.

Sadly and silently, Tatiana listens to this impassioned confession. Then she renders her final verdict. But how different is her rebuttal from that of Onegin's first lecture on a maiden's ethics! Hers are words permeated with sighs of a wounded heart:

> "Enough! Arise. I feel I must
> Reveal my thoughts for this may lessen
> Your pain. You will recall the day,
> When in the park, by fate's strange way,
> Together we were brought. Your lesson
> I then, alas! was doomed to learn.
> And yet, today, it is my turn.
> Onegin, then I was so youthful,
> And better then I was, maybe.
> I lovèd you, and I was truthful,
> But in your heart—what did I see?
> What was its answer?—Condemnation:
> A maiden's humble fascination,
> Her love, to you, were far from new."

And then Tatiana asks Onegin what petty whim had brought him to her feet: She suspects that he is more fascinated by the brilliant setting, in which he found her, than by anything that is truly part of her own self. To Tatiana the tinsel of her weary life, the frippery of the fatiguing masquerade are of no value or attraction. If it were only possible, she would gladly abandon all the splendor of her gleaming life

> "For silent bookshelves, dreamy parks,
> And our humble rural dwelling."

She tells Onegin that she still loves him, but having once pledged her loyalty to another, she must and will forever remain true to him.

Abruptly Poushkin draws the curtain, but before leaving his heroes to their fate, he heaves a sigh of regret, sounding a lamenting note on that which to himself was dear and yet had vanished, like a dream, into the all-engulfing Nirvana of the past:

>"But they to whom, at gath'rings gay,
>The early strophes I have read. . . .
>These are no more, those—far away,
>As Sádi once so aptly said.
>Without them was Onegin moulded.
>And thou, who hast to me unfolded
>Tatiana's beautiful ideal. . . .
>Yes, much did fate relentless steal! . . .
>Ah, happy he who early goes
>And leaves the feast of life divine,
>Who does not drain its cup of wine,
>Nor read its novel to the close,
>And swiftly parts with it, as I
>To my Onegin bade goodbye."

IX

PUSHKIN'S RELATION TO FOLKLORE
By MARTHA WARREN BECKWITH, PH.D.
Professor of Comparative Literature and Language, Vassar College

INTEREST in Pushkin for the folklorist takes two directions, one that of his contribution to the Russian national spirit, just awakening as the romantic movement swept the continent, and one that of his contribution to literature in the shape of folk and romantic fairytale translated into exquisite and immortal verse. It was not until 1855 that Afanasiev published his collection of Russian folk tales, almost twenty years after Pushkin's death. But Krylov's fables, called "the first imperfect revelation of nationality in Russian literature," had come out in 1809 and were widely read. Krylov had lived on the Volga and had caught up "turns of speech and mother wit" from its floating population which have since passed into proverb. Kirsha Danilov had brought out of complete obscurity the first collection of the Russian national epics which sang the exploits of Vladimir and his bogatyr. Joukovsky, poet and editor of the European Journal in Moscow, wrote ballads upon romantic fairytale themes and Pushkin's contemporary, Lermontov, was "embued with a love of folklore and knew history and popular tradition" and was hence able to "revive the atmosphere and color of mediaeval Russia." But it was Pushkin who, at the opening of the century, gave fullest expression to the awakening of the great Slavic empire to its national inheritance. Pushkin whose rebellious heart, when his pen was inexorably silenced by the official censor, still beat with affection and pity for the enslaved peasant. Pushkin who judged peasant and tsar by the same measure and believed that the retributive justice meted out in Russian folktale to those who oppressed the weak was in some way to be verified by fate.

Perhaps because he heard only French spoken in the family and learned his Russian as a second tongue among the people, Pushkin's use of it is native and vigorous and departs from artificial convention. Although he belonged to the aristocracy and entered into the society of the fashionable world, he loved to associate with the ruder sort. He is said to have wandered with the gypsies and he liked to visit country fairs and "to mingle with the beggars who chanted . . . at the gates of the local monasteries." He realized the tragic outlook upon life of the peasant folk. He was familiar with their songs and used them in his story of "The Captain's Daughter" to capture the intense spiritual outlook upon fate which finds

RELATION TO FOLKLORE 189

expression in the mournful boatman's song in which the captured outlaw, who has cast in his lot with wild nature and has cut himself off from the life of towns, sings—

> "Murmur not, mother forest of rustling green leaves,
> Hinder not a brave lad thinking his thoughts."

He wrote down folksongs from the lips of the people, marriage songs, dirges, and other songs belonging to folk ritual. The publication of sixteen Serbian folksongs translated into a meter based upon Russian folk epic, although he was deceived by Prosper Merimée's adroit imitations and included them as genuine in his collection called "Songs of the Western Slavs," is nevertheless evidence of his interest in the subject and his power to evoke the true flavor of Slavic folksong.

It is this power of Pushkin to realize imaginatively, to take delight, and to convey that delight to others, in what was true of Russian life outside his own aristocratic circle, to which Dostoyevsky pays tribute in a famous passage translated by Maurice Baring:

> "He accepted the people's truth as his truth. In spite of the people's vices, in spite of their evil and deadly habits, he was able to discern the existence of the greatness of the soul of the people, at a time when they entirely escaped almost everybody's notice, and he set up the popular ideal in his heart as his own ideal."

The periods of escape from the artificial life of fashionable society to some quiet country estate, such as that in the country at Boldino before his marriage in 1831, are among the most productive of his life. It was during his banishment to the family estate at Mikhaylovskoye in the province of Pskov between 1824 and 1826 that he heard from the lips of his nurse, old Arina Rodionovna, the folktales and legends of the Russian people which may well have shaped his narrative style.

Literature would be poorer without the five narrative poems, so graceful and flawless in architecture and phrasing, in which Pushkin retells five fairytales, all, with one exception, among the most popular and widespread types which have passed from mouth to mouth among both learned and unlearned throughout Europe and Asia. Of the two taken from Grimm's collection, although read by Pushkin in a French translation, both closely resemble the Grimm version.

In "The Fisherman and His Wife," * written in 1833 and printed in 1835, Pushkin tells how the poor fisherman catches a golden fish from the blue sea, but lets it go again in answer to its plea, refusing to take advantage of its offer to grant whatever reward he may ask. His wife, however, chides him for a fool and sends him back to ask for a new trough, her own having been lately broken. Ambi-

* "The Russian Wonderland." Translated by Boris Brasol. Paisley Press.

RELATION TO FOLKLORE 191

tion mounts with the easy granting of the first wish, and again and again the poor fisherman is driven back to the shore, first for a wooden house and garden, then a castle where she may live as lady, then as queen in a palace, finally as empress over the blue sea with the fish to serve as her messenger. At this the patience of the benefactor is exhausted. Wind and sea arise, and amidst the roar of thunder and the crash of waves upon the shore the magic edifice disappears and the fisherman turns home to find his wife sitting in the same old hovel as at first.

The motive itself is an old one. A Japanese accumulative story, quoted by Bolte and Polivka in their commentary upon Grimm's tales, tells of a discontented stonecutter who aspires to become the strongest in the world. An obliging deity changes him first into the sun, then a cloud, then a stone cliff; when, seeing a stonecutter attack the cliff with his iron tool, he is content to return to his original condition. In some early German dialect versions the fisherman goes home to consult his wife before voicing his wish or is even himself the aspirant, finally, to become God. In these dialogue forms he is given a folk name like Hans Entende, little man Domine, or Hans Dundledee with his wife Dinderlinde. In the Grimm version the man's call to the fish is in verse form and his wife is named Isabel, but Pushkin's couple are without this folk element. The wishes too, include the ambition to become, first the Pope, finally God himself, and command the sun and moon to rise and set. Such allusions, had Pushkin wished to employ them, would hardly have passed the censor. Pushkin's rendering makes for selection and economy in the use of detail. The incident of the broken trough seems to be his own invention; it does not appear in Grimm. He takes advantage, however, of the reiterative element in the Grimm text which so well conveys the effect of a nagging woman. He makes use, too, of the ominous note of warning as the sea changes and darkens and grows wilder at each return of the baffled fisherman. Both texts present the picture of a contented man overriden by an ambitious wife. It is hardly conceivable that Pushkin did not have his own case in mind when he composed this outwardly innocent fable.

In the story of the "Tsar's Daughter and the Seven Bogatyr," which he composed during the fertile period of literary composition in 1831 and published in 1832, Pushkin retells the familiar fairytale of Snow-white, perhaps with reference to his own love affair with the lady who at this time became his wife. The story, hence, although it follows closely Grimm's framework, differs widely in detail. The princess is a tsar's daughter. It is at her betrothal feast that the jealous new wife of the tsar consults her mirror and discovers her rival; the lover is thus introduced by name early in the story. It is a lady's maid and not a huntsman

RELATION TO FOLKLORE 193

who takes the girl into the forest (as in the similar episode in Tristrem and Isolt) and the savage incident of the salting and eating of the supposed victim's heart is omitted. It is not to the house of the German dwarfs that the girl comes in the forest, but to that of seven huge-bodied heroes of Russian folk epic, the followers of Vladimir. The scene lacks the childish dialogue formula endeared to children in the nursery tale of Goldilocks and the three bears and which occurs in the Grimm text. When the bogatyr return at night there is a clash of steel, a waving of moustaches, and a united shout of amazement goes up as they see the order which their visitor has brought about in the house. Emphasis is placed once more upon the absent lover in a pretty scene in which the eldest of the seven offers to make the girl his wife and all take her for sister when she explains her former betrothal. The jealous tsarina dressed as a beggar makes but one visit to the house in the forest. She does not gain entrance against the warning of the girl's protectors, as in the Grimm text, but tosses her a poisoned apple, one bite of which causes her to fall senseless. Here a new motive is introduced from some source, perhaps Russian, in which the faithful hound Sakolka does all that a dog can do to prevent her receiving the apple, finally swallowing himself the remainder of the fruit and dying by her side. As in the Grimm tale, the mourning brothers place the girl's lifeless form, fresh as in life, in a crystal casket, rest it upon six round pillars, bind it about with six iron bands to prevent its being stolen away, and hide it in a cavern underground. Her lover wanders disconsolate seeking his bride. He asks the sun, the moon, the wind after her who is the most beautiful on earth. The wind gives him the clue and, following a crevice underground, he recognizes his bride and gives such a blow upon the casket that the glass breaks. The girl awakes, rubs her eyes, wonders over the long nap she has had (a scene rationalized in some versions by giving the body a jolt which causes the bit of apple to fly out of her mouth). The tsarina dies of rage. The wedding feast is celebrated with a splendor such as never was on earth or in heaven. "I was myself at the feast, invited like the rest of the guests. I drank mead and beer but only just wet my whiskers." So the story ends as all Russian folktales conclude, as if the story-teller might thereby bring his listeners back from dreams of fairy times and places to the reality of here and now. Perhaps, too, there is a sly hint of himself as the prospective bridegroom.

The story seems to be descended from the Greek myth of Persephone, retold to fit into popular romantic fiction of the day. The queer conceit of the glass coffin placed within a chasm underground, resting on six pillars and bound about by six iron bands, certainly derives from the six months during which the Greek girl was bound to the under-

RELATION TO FOLKLORE 195

world, and the single bite of the poisoned apple is the pomegranate seed that Persephone swallowed, which condemned her to the realms of death. Perhaps Sakolka's prototype is the dog Cerberus, although we are nowhere in Greek myth given so kindly a view of the relations of that mythical monster with those who stray near the borders of the land of death. Such questions of comparative mythology, however, are far from Pushkin's interest in the story. His special inclination is to eliminate conventional motives and to give reality to scenes which interest him in the story as essentially human situations. The romantic motive of the wish-child "white as snow, red as blood, black as ebony" with which Grimm's text opens, is replaced by the touching picture of the pregnant mother watching the snow fall during the long winter months, until her husband returns on the same Christmas day on which God sends her a lovely daughter, and with this double joy her life ends. There is an air of comfortable human living about the description of the bogatyr's house in the forest; she knows by the holy pictures on the wall that good folk dwell there. There are lovely descriptions such as Pushkin delights in of the rivals' beauty; of the proud tsarina lifting her white shoulders before the glass and the marvelous blooming of the gentle, dark-haired daughter, "so lovely of countenance that no woman is her equal" says the steadfast mirror. Even the supernatural elements of the story are so subdued as to seem mere symbols of human realities. The magic glass is the mirror of the jealous woman's own mind which comes to realize the younger woman's beauty; the magic sleep is the death in life of a young maid's body until awakened by a true lover. Even more famous as a re-creation of a fairytale type is the story of Tsar Saltan * easily to be recognized as a variant of the "Three Golden Apples" (Grimm, number 96) of Antti Aarne's analysis. Three girls prattle of what they would do if the Tsar made them his wife. One would cook him a feast, one would weave him fine cloth, but the youngest would bear him a heroic son. The girls are overheard; the tsar places them in his palace. The first is made chief cook, the second chief spinner, the third he makes his wife. During his absence the wife bears him a noble son, but the jealous sisters conspire with the midwife Barbara to change the letters which pass between the two and pretend to the father that his wife has borne a monster, to the wife that her lord has condemned her to be fastened with her child in a cask and drowned in the sea. The cask, however, floats to an island in response to the child's wish-song and the boy Guidon, who has grown great by the hour instead of by the month like ordinary children, breaks open the cask and the two creep out upon

* "The Russian Wonderland." Translated by Boris Brasol. Paisley Press.

RELATION TO FOLKLORE

the shore. The boy makes a bow and arrow for himself and shoots an eagle which is pursuing a swan. This swan is no mere bird but an enchanted princess, daughter of the king of the sea. She builds him out of gratitude a splendid palace furnished with all things needful for a sumptuous life, and Guidon and his mother make it their home. Merchants come from over sea and carry to Tsar Saltan news of this marvel. He yearns to visit the island, but the sisters, fearful lest he discover their treachery, persuade nurse Barbara to describe, on three successive visits, three marvels each greater than the last. Each time the boy Guidon has, through the swan's connivance, flown with the ship in the form of a gnat to his father's home and overheard the wonder described. Each time the swan finds him downcast without this new marvel. The first is a red fir-tree under which sits a squirrel cracking nuts in time to a song, and every shell is made of gold and every kernel is an emerald. The second is a host of thirty heroes of giant stature who, at an appointed hour, spring all together out of the waves of the sea. The last is a maiden who lives beneath the sea, with a voice like the murmur of springs on the mountains and beauty that outshines the sun and lights the earth at night. On her shoulders rests a moon and on her forehead a star. Each of these wonders the swan maiden brings to the palace on the island. The heroes are her own brothers and the maiden is the swan herself, who now takes human form and becomes Guidon's wife. The Tsar finally comes to visit the island, Barbara having exhausted her stock of wonders, and the three plotters are exposed and the mother and son restored to the husband and father. No savage element is allowed to mar this happy outcome; the evil-minded women are simply sent away in disgrace.

The tale of the Golden Cock,* dated September 20, 1834, but too suspect to the censor to appear in its present form, is an adaptation from the "Tale of the Arabian Astrologer" which appeared in Washington Irving's "Alhambra" and which Pushkin read in 1832 in a French translation. Tsar Dadon, harassed by foes in his old age who attack him on every hand, promises whatever treasure he may name to an Arabian astrologer who insures him peace by setting up a warning cock to give signal at the approach of an enemy. Quiet settles upon the land and the old Tsar rejoices. But suddenly the cock begins to crow and flap its wings. The oldest son sallies forth with an army in the direction in which the cock points. After an interval, the second son is sent out with another band. Finally the old Tsar himself musters his troops and himself takes the field. Nothing is to be seen but a silken pavilion pitched upon the plain, before which his two sons lie slain, each by

* "The Russian Wonderland." Translated by Boris Brasol. Paisley Press.

RELATION TO FOLKLORE 199

the other's hand, while around them lie their slaughtered armies fallen in support of their leaders. Consternation seizes the Tsar, but when there emerges from the tent a beautiful enchantress who leads him within, all is forgotten and the enamoured father brings her home in triumph to the palace. At this point up steps the astrologer and demands his boon in the shape of the lady. The Tsar puts on a bold front, gives a death blow to the eunuch at his side who has introduced the wizard, and refuses to surrender his prize. The necromancer utters no word, but the cock flaps its wings, descends from its perch upon the Tsar's head, gives him a peck on his skull which is instantly fatal, and the astrologer vanishes with the lady.

Pushkin handles his source very freely, simplifying detail but following the plot exactly. The satire is said to have been written during the time of his quarrel with Tsar Nicholas I over a court appointment which Pushkin felt jeopardized his dignity in his relations with his giddy young wife; and the pointed reference to the anonymity of the land and the might of its Tsar, together with the warning against the danger of quarreling with potentates, may well interpreted to refer to this affair. The incident of the death of the eunuch who has introduced the astrologer to the court and has been accordingly held in high favor may also have some significance, since otherwise it seems a superfluous detail in a story so carefully shorn of over-elaboration. The idea that the threatened danger to the kingdom lies in a silken pavilion pitched by an enchantress for the possession of whom a fratricidal conflict is waged and for whose sake the Tsar himself loses his sense of obligation and honor, is the kind of obscure innuendo that the harassed husband of a pretty flirt might well seize upon for satirical purposes. To the apologue itself, Chaucer's Pardoner's tale, also of oriental origin, bears a close resemblance. It is not easy to believe that Browning had not read Pushkin when he composed his nursery tale of the Pied Piper of Hamelin Town, although the similarity of treatment may be explained by the likeness in the situation.

The broad satire of "The Pope and his Workman Balda," dated probably in 1831, also met with censorship. It belongs to a widespread folktale type which goes under the name of the "Labor contract" and is attached in Grimm's collection to the story called "The Young Giant." A parsimonious pope (more properly to be translated "priest" in the Russian) makes a bargain with the workman Balda for a year's service, the man's only payment to be the privilege of giving three blows on the pope's own head. As the time draws near the master, who has had evidence of the fellow's strength, becomes alarmed and consults his wife, who advises that the fellow be sent to collect back

RELATION TO FOLKLORE 201

rent from the devils of the sea and, failing in this, can then be sent packing. Balda terrorizes the devils, wins by trickery and bluff in the trials of strength they propose, and returns with a bag of gold to demand his wages. Thus the stingy master carries an addled head for the rest of his life.

In folktale the story attaches to a bear's son or one who has gained strength by being suckled by a giant, a mermaid, or in some other supernatural fashion. In his youth he uses his strength in all sorts of troublesome ways. Sent to bring in wood, he uproots whole trees; sent to herd cattle, he allows wild beasts to devour them and then herds the wild beasts themselves into the byre. He hires himself to a miserly bailiff on similar terms as in this story and the frightened master seeks his destruction. Sent to clean out a well he catches upon his head the millstone rolled down to kill him and appears wearing it about his neck as a collar. Sent to grind corn at the devils' mill, from which no man escapes alive, he throws the devils about until they retreat in terror, an episode closely connected with the popular tale of "The Youth who did not know what Fear was," and was sent to pass three nights in a haunted house beset with spirits. Often these spirits appear in cat form, suggestive of the messenger imp in Pushkin's tale who begins to mew like a famished kitten.

The tricks by which Balda outwits the devils are, however, independent of these two types.

They resemble more nearly those by which Grimm's "Valiant Tailor" outwits the dull-witted giant who proposes tests of strength. Balda first terrorizes the devils into believing that unless they bring in the gold, the rope which he is twisting in his hands will be used to raise a storm and destroy them all. The race test he wins by proxy by the famous device of concealing one animal at the goal and starting out its exact counterpart as if to cover the track. Finally he plays another bluff in the throwing contest by cocking his eye at a cloud and pretending he is about to burst it over the devils' heads with his missile. Both these, the animal relay race and the bluff motive, are very old types, probably oriental in origin, for the racing trick occurs in the Buddhist birth stories, the Indian Jataka, and the other is common in Indian folktale. An amusing example is to be found among the American Sioux Indians, where the trickster frightens away a monster by pretending he is about to take down the crescent moon to use as a bow. The underlying idea is the popular folk motive of the triumph of the weak against the strong, wit pitted against brawn, gods contending with giants, the fox with the wolf, the man with his master, perhaps the poet with his censor.

As in his fairytales so here Pushkin uses the utmost economy in detail. He rationalizes the incidents which in the folktales incline toward the marvelous. His workman is just an ordinary stout

RELATION TO FOLKLORE 203

fellow who "works like seven." Balda teases the devils, but uses only natural means to outwit them. The blows he gives do not, as in the folktales, knock the master into the sky. Nevertheless the motive of the wager remains nebulous and the poet's reason for choosing a priest as the butt of the satire obscure.

No words about Pushkin in relation to folklore can be complete without at least calling attention to the lovely prologue to his first romantic handling of fairy material, the famous "Ruslan and Ludmila," the discussion of which is a subject too involved for this paper. The poetic romance was composed during his school days and completed in 1820, but the prologue was not added until five years later. In enchanting verse he describes the oak beside the sea, wound about with a golden chain, around which day and night a wise tomcat circles, with a song if to the right and a tale if to the left. Woven into the wonders of the place are to be found all those magical themes with which old Arina used to embellish her tales and which are familiar images of the Russian folk imagination. Nixies and wood fauns, footprints of many strange animals upon an uncut trail, a little house without windows or doors standing upon chicken legs, ghosts that haunt the woods and valleys, and on the long white shore thirty knights who spring out of the wave with their white-haired old uncle. A prince overcomes a king; a magician gives to a knight wings over forest and sea; a princess weeps in a tower, a grey wolf serves her faithfully; a witch's kettle moves of itself; a prince and a miser come to grief over gold. There one can sniff the air of Russian steppes, there too has the poet himself drunk mead, seen the oak beside the sea, and heard the wise cat tell many a tale.

X

POUSHKIN, HIS PLACE IN LETTERS
By Col. George V. Golokhvastoff

On January 29th, 1837, Poushkin died, and the literary world of Russia realized at once, that it had lost a great poet. The high regard in which Poushkin was held by his contemporaries is an eloquent testimony of the irresistible influence which his creative art exerted, even during his lifetime, over his countrymen's minds and hearts. But this recognition of Poushkin's greatness did not save him from a brief period of eclipse. During the second half of the 19th century, Russia began a period of social change, affecting her way-of-life, her habits of thought, and her literature. It was a period of great realism. Anyone who was not thinking, talking, or writing with a practical view in mind was out of order. Critics demanded that even poetry satisfy purely utilitarian needs. It was this trend, which made the critics tend to belittle the importance of Poushkin and his creative art.

Fortunately, this misconception of the nature of Poushkin's genius, this narrow interpretation of the very sense of his poetical work, did not last long. As early as 1880, on the occasion of the unveiling of a monument to Poushkin in Moscow, Dostoyevsky delivered a celebrated address, in which he not only extolled Poushkin's signal services to Russian literature, but also, with great feeling, characterized him as a poet who not only revealed and embodied the Russian spirit, but was also filled with the spirit of all mankind.

This address marked the beginning of Poushkin's return from oblivion, and by the time the centenary of his birth was celebrated with great solemnity by all of Russia in 1899, he had already been accorded complete and final recognition.

The builder of the Russian literary language and father of modern Russian literature has at last taken his permanent place as the spirit and guiding genius for the Russian culture of all time. Once again, his poetry captivates all Russian hearts; henceforth, Russian children, from their earliest years, will study his creative art, and the name of Poushkin is, in every Russian's mind, inseparably linked with the picture of a thoroughly national-poet of the people. His name re-echoes in every Russian hamlet, and is carried on the tongues of all the tribes and nationalities inhabiting that great Empire. Thus has Poushkin's own prophecy, which he sounded in the "Monument," one year before his death, been fulfilled.—

"My name shall travel all through Russia's vast domains
And ev'ry living tongue shall learn to call it"

HIS PLACE IN LETTERS 207

Since that anniversary 38 years have elapsed—the whole span of Poushkin's brief life. The new anniversary, the centenary of his death, is now being celebrated, and is a chance for the world to add fresh laurels to the unfading wreath of his glory, and to fulfill the second part of the prophecy made by Poushkin in the "Monument."

Actually, however, the Great Russian poet has not, until now, received much recognition beyond the borders of his own country. Not yet is he sufficiently appreciated in foreign critical literature. He has been chiefly studied by Russian students, and not by students of literature. The chief reason for this is the almost insurmountable difficulty of mastering the Russian language. The difficulties of language and translation having kept Poushkin more or less obscure to the world at large, it is more than time for someone to overcome these technical difficulties and to give us a thorough literary critique of Poushkin and his art. For his outlook and his philosophy were world embracing, and his great fund of original characters belongs psychologically to all the world, to all humanity. The need for such an endeavor is particularly great at present, as there is an ever growing interest in Russian literature, both in America and Europe. It is therefore essential that people studying Russian literature understand correctly its source—Poushkin.

Genius is not ashamed to learn from genius. And

no genius can properly be censured because of temporary outward influences, as long as his own works, the total of his creative art, rest on the two fundamental poles: originality and perfection. Such was the progress and the development of Poushkin's career.

No outside influences, no contact with other geniuses, held any danger to his spiritual powers, to his creative "ego." Just as great rivers receive smaller ones into their broad channels, and absorb them in their own powerful flow, so the creative Will in Poushkin was not subjugated to foreign influences, did not re-echo them, but, ever keeping its own independence, readapted them, using them in an ingenious way as an additional instrument for the achievement of highest perfection in his own, ever original work.

Poushkin realized many objectives; the vitalizing of Russian literature with the spirit of national individuality, the choosing of a right course for Russian literature, in the sense of formulating its artistic problems, and grounding it firmly in the broad meaning of art, also the comprehensive development of Russian literature, so as to make it not only a repository for all things Russian, but the possessor in its universal scope of all by which humanity lives.

Being widely acquainted with the new currents in the literature of other nations, Poushkin, at the outset of his poetic career, could not help noticing the backwardness of Russian literature, which had stopped at the threshold of Romanticism. He was offended by the artificiality and the false conception of beauty in the forms of prevalent sentimental literature. Nor was Poushkin's aesthetic credo fully satisfied with the general level of Western-European romanticism. He did not consider romanticism of this pattern, expressive of true art; he saw in it just a passing, and, therefore, conventional trend.

This leads us to ask what Poushkin desired of creative writing, and what gods it should serve, if any. Also what were the qualities which made up the perfection of his art, which placed it so far above the level of his time, that not only his contemporaries, but even subsequent generations have been unable to appreciate the poet's mastership in all its harmonious perfection.

Perhaps Belinsky sheds light on the problem, when he says that Poushkin is preeminently an artist, not only in verse, but also in feeling; and that his poetry, as art without relation to contents, is both its own goal, and the fount of an influence which ennobles the human soul. But further, we have seen that Poushkin, without deviating from the laws of aesthetics, has saturated his poetry with lofty thought and powerful sentiment, thus satisfying all intellectual and moral aspirations of the human soul.

Poushkin wanted most of all to re-create Russian

literature, this at a time when that of all other great nations was already formed and mature—he wanted it to serve Russian speech and Russian culture, under the banner of a lofty ideal, embodying the beauty and truth of universal art. But he knew the secret of artistic equilibrium, for in his works the principles of the intellectually moral and of the aesthetic, blend in perfect harmony in an easy and natural manner. Perhaps not jokingly at all, Poushkin, with his peculiar epigrammatic quality, once made the remark: "Poetry, the Lord forgive us, should be not too learned. . . ." In the light of a comprehensive study of Poushkin's creative art, this paradox is not only of exceptional interest, but contains, possibly, the key to a further understanding of Poushkin, and to a whole number of controversial subjects, related to the general concepts of poetry and the rôle of a poet.

We must not be led by this last remark into thinking that Poushkin was not a realist, as some of his critics wrongly believed. For throughout Poushkin's poetry, we consistently find the human mind in full harmony with the laws of the external world, with human thought, with the mysteries of nature and the human heart, and with the fluctuating conditions of life.

There is no warping of the soul in Poushkin, no psychological dualism; he does not entangle himself in the meshes of fate, does not fret his wounded heart with idle doubts. True, among his lighthearted, almost childishly joyous motifs, we find not a few lyrical themes, some of them warm with soft sorrow, others filled with deep grief, still others breathing sincere regrets. But in all these emotions expressed by Poushkin, there is no morbid despondency, so characteristic of most poets of "inner Emotions." His fundamental quality is a completely healthy spiritual contentment. This makes his thought clear and lucid, and his sentiment unaffectedly truthful in its entirety; it creates a continuous fount of artistic enjoyment.

The multivoiced appeals of life, and the eternal mystery of nonentity, greatness, and obscurity, heroic feats, and villainy, friendship and enmity, the many-faced human joys and fears, and love in its infinite variations,—all these have been immortalized by Poushkin with that truthfulness and feeling, which once more stamp his creative art as belonging to all humanity.

The sunny quality of Poushkin's genius is a phenomenon wonderful to behold and one which may perhaps never repeat itself. Even the mighty Goethe, that "great pagan," with his lofty olympic calm, makes rather an impression of one initiated into some high order, and who has achieved an imperturbable spiritual equilibrium as a result of wisdom, and through the conquest of life and the universe by an eminent effort of his will. But not so with Poushkin; he, Russia's qualified successor of the antique world, loved the universe, as well as life and people, through his own serenity, which was also the source of his whole wisdom.

Poushkin consciously tried to reveal his literary "credo" in a cycle of poems: "The Muse," "The Prophet," "Conversation of a Poet with a Bookseller," and "The Poet." This cycle takes the poet through a long range of emotions and conflicts,— in "The Prophet," he gives the picture of a poet being chosen by divine power, which causes his spiritual rebirth, necessary for a fulfillment of the sacred duty entrusted to him, "to set afire, with words, the human heart."

In "Conversation of a Poet with a Bookseller," we find the conflict of creative power, with the abasement of material dependence, and the weakness of human disillusionment, in the fact that the poet's dreams, which are warmed by his love of men, find no response among "the thoughtless rabble."

In "The Poet," the discord in the contact of two alien worlds is solved. In it the calm consciousness of the immutability of universal laws is reconciled with the poet's nature, the worldly duality of the inspired elect of heaven, and the poor worldly-vain sons of earth are in accord. Perhaps no one has felt this fatal dualism as keenly, as did Poushkin himself, for, in Tiutcheff's definition, "He was a living organ of the gods . . . but full of blood, of boiling blood. . . ."

Added to this group of poems, dedicated to the

philosophy of the conception and function of the poetic art, is a second group which corresponds to it, in that they are a poetic expression of the ideas previously expressed. To this group belong "Echo," "The Rabble," and the sonnet "To a Poet."

It is evident that the definitions of poetry and poet in the poem "Echo," correspond to an intellectually moral approach to Poetry. In the ingeniously simple and inexpressibly melodious lines of four-metered iambic, in which the recurring monotonousness of rhyme seems to imitate the repeated resounds of an echo, Poushkin likens the poet, and, through him, poetry, to just such a sensitive echo, responsive to the thunder of heaven, the scream of the eagle in the skies, the rumble of the ocean waves, the simple-hearted chant of the shepherd, the soft tunefulness of a maid singing, the call of the hunting horn, and the roar of the wild beast in its forest thicket. Can this be called indifference, or ignoring the realities of life, or shunning all interests outside art? Poushkin believes that the poet must and does, like an echo, respond to all problems of the world, all manifestations of nature, and all happenings of life.

But we also find in his poem, "The Rabble," a poet's firmly proud refusal to turn poetry into a moral sermon, with useful lessons for the correction of human errors and vices. And with that spiritual serenity, so characteristic of him, Poushkin concludes his admonition with the sublime acknowledgment that poets are born, "not for earthly agitation, not for gain or battle grounds" but only, "for inspiration, rev'rend prayers, and sweet sounds."

It may be that great poets are born rather than made. Nevertheless, there is nothing accidental in verse—its masters are necessarily wholly conscious of the technique of their medium. Of none of the world's great poets was this more deeply true than of Poushkin. He understood with the utmost exactitude the underlying principles of his art, and it is this knowledge, as exemplified in all his verse, which may well prove to be his most lasting monument.

Not content with his contribution to letters in this, as in so many respects, some have brought against him the reproach that he was no innovator; and further that he felt no great interest in politics. The first accusation is too palpably absurd to be worth noticing. The second is almost equally ill-founded. As a poet, Poushkin felt it his privilege to sound deeply such notes as interested him, and to reject the rest. He was no politician; but he had quite definite moral, social and political views, and his verse is full of them. "The Dagger," the "Ode to Liberty" and many other poems furnish evidence enough of his patriotism, and healthy nationalism. That he was insufficiently utilitarian to please Belinsky and his followers, is

HIS PLACE IN LETTERS 215

rather a demonstration of the limitations of his critics, than a slur upon the poet. Poushkin was Poushkin—the world has found it sufficient!

Passing enthusiasms for short-lived popular favorites like Nekrassoff signify little in the fullness of time. Nekrassoff is almost forgotten while Poushkin looms larger than ever. As he demonstrates in his "Monument," he is the poet of "mighty thoughts" and of the eternal spirit of man's stubborn striving towards perfection. As he states in this confession of faith, he stood for tenderness, for liberty, and for mercy. He did not boast, but he felt, as all great men must, a calm consciousness of his own merits. From his early youth, these qualities were actively evident in his poetic writings; and he may be credited with a real share in the eventual abolition of serfdom, and a growing measure of general personal freedom. Thus Poushkin, thinker and poet in one, achieved his high objective in the growth of freedom. In the noble figure of the nomad gypsy, Zemphira's father, Poushkin gave the civilized world, once and for all time, the supreme image of his high ideal of Liberty. With that, let his critics rest content!

With his sunny art, he rendered equal service to his favorite causes of tenderness and mercy; and as poet, psychologist, dramatist, and thinker, amply justifies the appellation so generally awarded to him of the Russian Shakespeare. All these qualities are particularly evident in the extraordinary condensation of his one-act plays, exemplifying as they do Boileau's fundamental rule: "Let speech be crowded, and let thought have room." In these miniature dramas, the action grows naturally, develops freely, and is unvaryingly accurate in psychology. Their brilliant form and enchanting beauty are unmatched and unmatchable. "Mozart and Salieri" and "Don Juan," short as they are, are masterpieces in miniature, and completely successful in their own peculiar genre. As Dostoyevsky pointed out in his famous eulogy, Poushkin shows here, as elsewhere, the unique gift of entering into the spirit of men of other nations, as no poet before or since has ever done. Quite likely his historical sense, and his practice in historical writing, helped him to make his Spaniards Spanish, his Teutons German, to a degree not approached by Shakespeare himself.

In conclusion, let us point out that, in the relatively small number of his dramatic works, Poushkin covers the whole range of human emotions. None are omitted—all are dealt with to the utmost.

Poushkin, the thinker and psychologist, has keenly eyed, as if from an unattainable spiritual height, the whole of life to the farthest horizon, and has caught in it all the reflections of the human soul. His creative art, in all the multiplicity of thought, sentiment, and images, reflects the soul with such immortal truth as if he had himself lived all of human life. Not without reason did a contemporary poet stress the manysided versatility of Poushkin's realization of life and the universe, by christening him "Proteus."

XI

ANTHOLOGY

The Talisman

WHERE fierce the surge with awful bellow
  Doth ever lash the rocky wall,
And where the moon most brightly mellow
  Doth beam when mists of evening fall;
Where midst his harem's countless blisses
  The Moslem spends his vital span,
A sorceress there with gentle kisses
  Presented me a Talisman.

And said: "Until thy latest minute
  Preserve, preserve my Talisman;
A secret power it holds within it,—
  'Twas love, true love the gift did plan.
From pest on land or death on ocean
  When hurricanes its surface fan,
O object of my fond devotion!
  Thou scap'st not by my Talisman.

"The gem in eastern mine which slumbers,
  Or ruddy gold 'twill not bestow;
'Twill not subdue the turbanned numbers
  Before the Prophet's shrine which bow;
Nor high through air on friendly pinions
  Can bear thee swift to home or clan,
From mournful climes or strange dominions,
  From South to North,—my Talisman.

"But oh! when crafty eyes thy reason
  With sorceries sudden seek to move,
And when in night's mysterious season
  Lips cling to thine,—but not in love,—
From proving then, dear youth, a booty
  To those who falsely would trepan,
From new heart wounds, and lapse from duty,
  Protect thee shall my Talisman."
                Translated by GEORGE BORROW.

The Poison-Tree

REMOTE and dire, in desert-lands
Where naught but sunburnt sod is seen,
Anchar, the Tree of Poison, stands—
A sentinel, with threatening mien.

The thirsty steppe-land gave it birth
In bitterness and anger dark;
It sucked foul venom from the earth,
Its roots and leaves are dead and stark.

At noon, when fiercest sunlight glows,
The poison from its veins escapes,
And trickling down the stem it flows
By evening into globed shapes.

No bird will seek this Tree of Death,
Nor dare the tiger prowl anigh,
The hungry whirlwind's dusty breath
Glows baneful as it hastens by.

If e'er a wand'ring cloud distil
Soft rains upon its blighted top,
Their harmless nature turns to ill,
And changed, in deadly dews they drop.

But yet a man's imperial nod
Sent forth a fellow-man afar,
Whose meek, obedient footsteps trod,
Right to the base of foul Anchar.

By morning he returned, and bore
The fatal resin, with a bough
Of withered leaves, and like it wore
A wasted look—and from his brow

Cold sweat was streaming, and he tried
To stand, but fell to earth prostrate.
And there, poor slave! he sank and died
In presence of the Potentate,

Who sopped his arrows in the bane,
And sent them dark—a doom new-found!—
By messenger o'er hill and plain
To neighbours in the countries round.

Translation by CHARLOTTE SIDGWICK, *Free Russia,*
January, 1899.

I do not long for you

I DO not long for you, years of my spring,
Which dreams of idle love have only wasted!
I do not long for you, mysterious nights,
Praised by a songstress who all passion tasted!

I do not long for you, unfaithful friends,
The crowns of feasts, the cups that pass around;
I do not long for you, young traitresses!—
In sadness, far from all of you I'm bound.

But where are you, ye moments of delight,
Of youthful hopes, when hearts in silence sing,
Where is the former warmth and inspiration?
Come back again to me, years of my spring!

The Angel

AT EDEN's gates an angel holy
  Was shining with bowed reverent head,
While o'er the abyss of hell soared slowly
  A demon with black pinions dread.

The rebel spirit of doubt and lying
  Beheld the sinless one; and then
The glow of tenderness, fast dying,
  Awoke within his breast again!

"Farewell! my eyes have seen the vision;
  Thou dost not shine in vain!," he cries.
"Not all on earth draws my derision,
  Not all in heaven do I despise!"
Translated by NATHAN HASKELL DOLE.

To his friend, Pushchin

MY OLDEST friend, my friend most true!
I truly blessed a kindly fate,
When to my home, now known to few,
And barred by snow, the sad winds blew
Your sleigh bells, pealing at my gate.

I pray unto a holy Fate
That in your soul my voice may stay
As pure delight and comfort great,
And lighten your unhappy state
With beams of our bright Lyceum day.

To Mme. Kern

Yes! I remember well our meeting,
  When first thou dawndest on my sight,
Like some fair phantom past me fleeting,
  Some nymph of purity and light.

By weary agonies surrounded,
  'Mid toil, 'mid mean and noisy care,
Long in mine ear thy soft voice sounded,
  Long dreamèd I of thy features fair.

Years flew; Fate's blast grew ever stronger,
  Scatt'ring mine early dreams to air,
And thy soft voice I heard no longer—
  No longer saw thy features fair.

In exile's silent desolation
  Slowly dragg'd on the days for me—
Orphan'd of life, of inspiration,
  Of tears, of love, of deity.

I woke—once more my heart was beating—
  Once more thou dawndest on my sight,
Like some fair phantom past me fleeting,
  Some nymph of purity and light.

My heart has found its consolation—
  All has revived once more for me—
And vanish'd life, and inspiration,
  And tears, and love, and deity.

Translated by THOMAS B. SHAW.

To his wife

'Tis time, my friend 'tis time! My heart now craves
   for rest.
The days fly by apace, and every day distressed
Takes off a part of life; together you and I
Are planning still to live. All is but dust, we'll die!
There is no happiness, there's freedom and repose,
I long have dreamed myself of banishing these woes.
I long, a tired slave, have hoped to take my flight
Unto a distant home of toil and pure delight.

V.

October nineteenth, 1831

Each time our own Lycee doth meet
To celebrate its natal day,
More and more timidly old friends
Join in one family, as they may—
More rarely one another greet.
Dark shadows flit across the board,
Duller do sound the greeting cups
Sadder our songs in their accord.

Friends of days past, 'tis twenty years
Since that great day of which I tell.
The tsar who ruled us is no more,
We burned down Moscow, Paris fell,
Bonaparte's dead in exile drear;
The fame of ancient Greece revives,
Another Bourbon's left his throne,
Revolt again in Warsaw thrives.

The blasts of all these earthly storms
Have touched us too, despite our will
To linger midst the feasts of youth,
And turn our ears from bodings ill.
We've grown mature; fate hath decreed
The trials of life that we must share.
Death's spirit grim has breathed on us,
And taken some we scarce can spare.

Six empty chairs surround our board,
Bereft of friends we'll see no more:
Wide scattered now, in peace they sleep,
Who graced our gatherings of yore.
One lies at home, one rests afar,
A third succumbed to sickness drear,
A fourth died of a broken heart—
Now over each we'll shed a tear.

I wonder if my own turn's next?
My lost friend Delvig calls to me—
The comrade of my youth unvexed,
My friend in sadness, and in glee.
My comrade in the songs of youth,
Its feasts and thoughts so passing fair—
That genius lost from out our midst
Calls me to join the spirits there.

Draw nearer, friends of olden days,
Form a small circle, while we learn
To the dear dead to bid farewell,
That we may to the living turn,
With hope that all again may meet
At the loved feast of the Lycee,
And one another gladly greet,
Fearless, upon this festal day.
      Anonymous.

Mozart and Salieri

Scene I

Room in Salieri's house

Salieri—

It has been told; there is no truth on Earth
There's none in Heaven either. To my mind
It is as plain as any simple scale,
I have loved Art since days of tender childhood;
When high above my head the organ sounded
In days of yore in our ancient church.
I listened then in rapture, and my eyes
Were filled with sweet involuntary tears.
I early spurned the futile games of youth,
All that to Music foreign was, it seemed
Distasteful to my proud and stubborn mind.
And I renounced it all, devoting all my heart
To Music only. The first step was hard,
And the beginning dull. I overcame
The early hardships. Handicraft I placed
Deep at the bottom of the holy Art;
A handicraftsman I became. My fingers
I trained into a fluent, dry technique.
Dissecting Music like a corpse, I killed
Misleading sounds, and tested harmony
With Algebra. And having thus explored
The very depths of the unerring science
I dared indulge in sweet creative dreams.
I started to create in secret only,
At first not even daring dream of fame.
How often after having spent in silence
Two or three days, forgetting sleep and food
And testing joy and tears of inspiration,
I burned my work and witnessed in cold blood

How sounds and thoughts, the children of my soul
In flames and fleeting smoke were fast consumed.
What do I say? When the immortal Gluck
Appeared and brought to us the revelation
Of new and fascinating mysteries
Did I not thrust aside my former knowledge,
Beloved and worshipped with such ardent faith?
Did I not follow him without a murmur
With new found energy, as one
Who lost his way and saw a guiding light?
Through forceful, unrelenting perseverance
I reached within the boundless realm of Art
A high perfection. Fame bestowed its smile
Upon my works. Within the hearts of men
I found a quick response to my creations.
I tested happiness, enjoyed in peace
My own successful work, as well as
The work and the success of many friends
Who were my mates in the pursuit of art.
I've never known the pangs of jealousy
I was not jealous even when Piccini
Enchanted the untutored ear of Paris.
I felt no envy when I first beheld
The solemn sounds of Iphigenia
And who would dare reproach the proud Salieri
Of envy or of petty jealousy,
Of being a trodden vicious worm that wriggles
Devouring dust and sand in helpless rage?
No one would dare, and yet I must confess,
To-day I'm jealous, yes, I envy deeply,
I'm tortured now by jealousy, Oh Heaven.
Where is thy Justice when a holy gift,
When the undying genius is bestowed
Upon the head of an unworthy loafer,
A dissipated fool! instead of being

The just reward for an undying flame,
Of abnegation, work and perseverance . . .
>   (MOZART *enters.*)
Mozart—
Ah! So you saw me! And I had in mind
To treat you unawares to a burlesque!
Salieri—
Where do you come from?
Mozart—
>   On my way to you
I passed a dingy tavern, and I heard
The screechy sound of an old violin. . . .
I say! Salieri! You have never heard
In all your blessed life a thing so funny:
A blind old fiddler in the midst of drunkards
Played with much gusto my *Vio che sapete*.
I could not overcome the great temptation
And brought the fiddler here. You'll have some fun!
Come in!
>   *(A blind fiddler enters.)*
>   Play now for us something by Mozart.
The fiddler plays the aria from Don Jovanni.
MOZART *roars with laughter.*
Salieri—
And you can laugh:
Mozart—
>   Great God, my dear Salieri!
How can you help enjoy this perfect joke?
Salieri—
I can't enjoy it when a clumsy bungler
Besmirches boldly Raphael's Madonna,
I see no banter when a mountebank
By parodies dishonors Alighieri.
>   *(To the fiddler.)*
Get out, old fool.

Mozart—
>Wait, take this here from me,
Drink to the health of Mozart.
>*(Exit old fiddler.)*
>Dear Salieri,
You seem to have the blues. I will come later
And show you something.
Salieri—
>What is it you brought?
Mozart—
Oh really nothing, just a foolish trifle.
Last night somehow I could not fall asleep.
A few ideas came into my mind.
I jotted down the melody to-day
And came to you to ask for your opinion
But since you're indisposed . . .
Salieri—
>Oh . . . Mozart! Mozart!
I always am disposed to hear your music.
Sit down and play.
Mozart (at the piano)—
>Imagine now someone . . .
Imagine me . . . perhaps a little younger,
In love, not over deeply, but enough;
And chatting gaily with a friend; with you
For instance . . . Then a sudden ghastly vision,
A clammy darkness . . . or that sort of thing.
Now listen here . . .
>*(He plays.)*
Salieri—
>You came to play me *that*
And yet you could have lingered at the tavern,
And listened to the fiddler's parody!
You Mozart, are unworthy of yourself!

Mozart—
Well? Is it good?
Salieri—
What a prophetic depth!
What daring, and withal what harmony!
You are divine and do not even know it,
It's I who know . . .
Mozart—
          No really? Well perhaps,
But my divinity is very hungry.
Salieri—
How would the *Golden Lion* suit your fancy?
A dinner and a jug of wine?
Mozart—
        I'm game
But first I'd better go and tell my wife
That she should not expect me home for dinner.
Salieri—
Be sure to come. I'll see you at the tavern.
                      (Exit MOZART.*)*
Oh, no! I can resist my fate no longer,
I'm destined to stop him. Otherwise
We all must perish, all of us who are
High priests before the holy shrine of Music.
Not I alone bereft of just reward.
What good is it if Mozart stays alive?
And even if he reaches greater heights?
He will not lift the plane of art forever,
It will slip back once he has passed away.
No one will have the force to take his place.
What good is he? A kind of Cherubim
He brought to us some songs from Paradise
Arousing futile hopes and helpless longing
In us who have no wings. Let him go back
To Heaven whence he comes, and rest in peace. . . .

This deadly drug, a gift from my Isora
I've cherished many years. How many times
Did life appear unbearable to me!
How often with a careless enemy
Have I not sat together at a meal . . .
And never did I yield to the temptation.
Although I've never been a coward, neither,
And I impervious to grave offence.
Nor have I fear of death. I bade my time
Whenever welcome death appeared to me,
Why die? I thought, when life may yet bestow
Upon me new and unexpected gifts;
Perhaps I would be blessed by heavenly rapture,
Creative dreams or God sent inspiration;
Perhaps some other Haydn would create
Some new and greater music for my ears.
And when I feasted with an enemy
I thought: perhaps a still more hated foe
I soon should meet; perhaps a worse insult
Would cry to Heaven for a just revenge,
Then will I need thee, my Isora's gift!
And I was right: And now at last I found
My greatest enemy, and a new Haydn
Enraptured me with pure and heavenly joy.
The hour has struck. Thou blessed gift of love,
To-day thou passest in the cup of friendship.

Scene II

(Private room in an inn; a piano, Mozart and Salieri at table.)

Salieri—
You seem disturbed to-day?
Mozart—
        Oh no, I'm not.

Salieri—
But surely you look troubled my dear friend.
A toothsome meal, the best of Burgundy,
And you are dull and mute . . .
Mozart—
              I must confess
It is my Requiem that galls me.
Salieri—
What made you, pray! compose a *Requiem?*
Mozart—
It happened weeks ago . . . A strange event
Did I not tell you?
Salieri—
          No.
Mozart—
              It was like this:
About three weeks ago, one night when I
Was coming home, they told me that a man
Had called upon me, and all thru the night
I wondered who that stranger might have been
And what was the intention of his errand.
He came again and did not find me home.
Another day, when I was on the floor
Engaged in playing with my little boy,
The caller came again, all clad in black.
He asked me then to write a Requiem.
I set to work as soon as he had left;
And since that day the visitor in black
Has not come back to claim the finished work.
I'm really glad, since I am loath to part
With it, although the Requiem is ready.
However something tells me . . .
Salieri—
What is it?

Mozart—
I feel reluctant to confess . . .
Salieri—
     But what?
Mozart—
My visitor in black disturbs my thoughts
And follows all my steps by day and night
Like some mysterious shadow. Even now
I feel his presence here, with us, at table.
Salieri—
Why Mozart! What a childish, futile fear!
Shake off thy gloomy thoughts. Friend Beaumarché
Has often said to me: "My dear Salieri,
Whenever you are troubled by black thoughts,
Uncork a bottle of French Champaigne, or else
Reread the Marriage of my Figaro."
Mozart—
That's right, you were a friend of Beaumarché's
You have composed the music for *Tarara*.
It is good music. There's a little tune
Which always comes into my memory
When I am happy; by the way, Salieri,
I heard that Beaumarché had poisoned someone.
You think it's true?
Salieri—
    Why no! It could not be
He was too gay for such a deed.
Mozart—
     Besides
He was a genius, just like you and me;
And genius can't be yoked with murder. Can it?
Salieri—
You think it can't?
    (*He throws poison in* Mozart's *glass.*)
    Let's have a drink.

Mozart—
>Your health!
I drink this for our friendship, for the ties
Which link together Mozart and Salieri,
Who both are sons of Harmony . . .
Salieri—
>Hold on!
Stop, wait for me . . . you drank your glass too soon.
Mozart—*(throws his napkin on the table.)*
I'm thru.
>*(Goes over to the piano.)*
Now listen to my Requiem.
>*(He plays the Requiem.)*
You're crying?
Salieri—
>I have never cried before
As I am crying now. My tears are sweet
And bitter all at once. I feel as if
I had performed a painful duty. Or
As if a healing knife had cut from me
Some poisoned flesh. Dear Mozart, never mind
Those tears. Continue, hurry, I implore you
To fill my soul with more enrapturing sounds.
Mozart—
If only everybody had the power
To feel like you the spell of harmony!
But no. The world could then exist no more!
Since nobody would care for earthly needs
And all would want to serve immortal Art.
We are but few, we chosen happy idlers
Despising petty gain and low advantage,
High priests of heavenly Art. Am I not right?
I don't feel well to-day, I have some fever
My head is dull. I'd better go to sleep,
Farewell my friend!

Salieri—
Farewell
                                    (*Exit* Mozart.)
Your sleep will be
A long one Mozart . . . What if he is right?
And "genius can't be yoked with murder?" Am I
Perhaps no genius? Nonsense! How about
The crime committed by Buonarotti?
But may it not be just a calumny? . . .
A lie! Perhaps the man who has created
The Vatican has never been a murderer.

   Translated by Nicholas Lubimov, "Poet Lore," v. 31.

The Demons

Clouds are shifting, clouds are flying,
  Scarce the hidden moon's pale light
On the drifting snow is lying,—
  Wild the heavens, wild the night.
Swiftly o'er the stormswept lowland—
  Jingle, jingle bells amain!
Swiftly still, though heavy-hearted,
  Drive I o'er the frozen main.

"Ho there! driver, onward!" "Faster,
  Good my lord, we may not go,
For the stormwind blinds me, master,
  And the road is choked with snow."
Useless all! the track is hidden;
  We are lost to help and home;
From afar the demon spies us—
  Closer circling see him come!

Ha! beside us he's careering,
  Hissing, spitting,—now, I ween,
Round the steeds so madly veering
  On the brink of yon ravine.
There—if near or far I know not—
  He was whirling in my sight.
There again he pined and dwindled,
  Vanished into empty night!

Clouds are shifting, clouds are flying,
  Scarce the hidden moon's pale light
On the drifting snow is lying—
  Wild the heavens, wild the night.
Courage fails to struggle longer,
  Suddenly the sleigh bells cease—
Stops the team—Declare thou yonder—
  Wolf or tree-stem—is it peace?

Hark, the wind is wailing sadly,
  Loudly snort the startled team.
There, see there, he gambols madly,
  Through the murk his eyeballs gleam.
Once again the team has started—
  Jingle, jingle bells amain!
Lo, the spirit-hosts assemble
  O'er the faintly gleaming plain!

Form they have not, have no number,
  Lightly whirling round, they seem
Like the dead leaves of November
  In the moon's uncertain beam.
Are they endless? whither fly they?
  Why this wailful chanting, say!
Mourn they now their dead? In marriage
  Give they, else, some witch away?

Clouds are shifting, clouds are flying,
  Scarce the hidden moon's pale light
On the drifting snow is lying,—
  Wild the heavens, wild the night.
Still they come and still they vanish
  In the darkness o'er the plain,
Still their moaning and imploring
  Rends my very heart in twain!

Translations by Miss H. Frank, *in The Anglo-Russian Literary Society,* No. 34.

BIBLIOGRAPHY

A. S. Pushkin in English

A selected list of works by and about A. S. Pushkin
Compiled by Helen A. Shenitz, M.A., B.S.L.S.

I. Collected Works Arranged Chronologically

The talisman, from the Russian of A. Pushkin, with other pieces. St. Petersburg, 1835. 8°. Translated by George Borrow.

Russian romance, by Alexander Serguevitch Poushkin. Translated by Mrs. J. Buchan Telfer (née Mouravieff). London: H. S. King and Co., 1875. 293 p. 8°.
Contents: The captain's daughter.—The lady-rustic.—The pistol-shot.—The snow-storm.—The under-taker.—The station master.—The moor of Peter the Great.

Translations from Russian and German poets by a Russian lady. 1875-1878. Baden-Baden: A. von Hagen, 1878. 80 p. 8°.

Poems, by Alexander Pushkin. Translated from the Russian, with introduction and notes, by Ivan Panin. Boston: Cupples and Hurd, 1888. 179 p. 16°.

The queen of spades, and other stories. By A. S. Pushkin. With a biography. Translated from the Russian by Mrs. Sutherland Edwards. Illustrated. London: Chapman & Hall, 1892. 8°.

The prose tales of Alexander Poushkin, translated from the Russian by T. Keane. London: G. Bell and Sons, 1896. 466 p. 16°.
Contents: The captain's daughter.—Doubrovsky.—The queen of spades.—An amateur peasant girl.—The shot.—The snowstorm.—The post master.—The coffin-maker.—Kirdjali.—The Egyptian nights.—Peter the Great's negro.

Translations from Poushkin in memory of the hundredth anniversary of the poet's birthday, by Charles Edward Turner. St. Petersburg [etc.]: K. L. Ricker, 1899. 328 p. front. port. 12°.

[Verses and prose.] In: Wiener, L. Anthology of Russian literature from the earliest period to the present time. New York [etc.]: G. P. Putnam's Sons, 1902-03. 2 v. fronts. ports. 8°. v. 2. p. 123-149.

List of author's works in English, v. 2. p. 123-125.

[Verses.] In: Newmarch, R. Poetry and progress in Russia. London: J. Lane, 1907. xvi, 269 p. front. ports. 8°. p. 112-127.

Contents: The black shawl.—The upas tree.—To A. P. Kern.—The talisman. Translated by W. R. Morfill.—The high road in winter.—The roussalka.—Eastern song.—Tatiana's letter, from "Eugene Oniegin." Translated by Rosa Newmarch.—The duel from Eugene Oniegin." Translated by H. C. F.

The prose tales of Alexander Poushkin. Translated from the Russian by T. Keane. London: G. Bell and Sons, Ltd., 1914. 466 p. 16°. (Bohn's popular library.)

Contents: The captain's daughter.—Doubrovsky.—The queen of spades.—An amateur peasant girl.—The shot.—The snowstorm.—The post master.—The coffin-maker.—Kirdjali.—The Egyptian nights. —Peter the Great's negro.

The prose tales of Alexander Poushkin. Translated from the Russian by T. Keane. London: G. Bell and Sons, Ltd., 1916. 466 p. 12°. (Bohn's standard library.)

Contents: The captain's daughter.—Doubrovsky.—The queen of spades.—An amateur peasant girl.—The shot.—The snowstorm.—The post master.—The coffinmaker.—Kirdjali.—The Egyptian nights. —Peter the Great's negro.

Three tales: The snowstorm; The postmaster; The undertaker; by A. S. Pushkin. Translated by R. T. Currall. Russian text accented by A. Semeonoff. London [etc.]: G. G. Harrap & Co., Ltd., [1919.] 56, 56 p. 16°. (Bilingual ser. Russian-English.)

Added t.-p. in Russian.

Text and translation on opposite pages.

[Verses.] In: Champney, Mrs. Elizabeth and F. Champney. Romance of Russia, from Rurik to bolshevik, by Elizabeth W. Champney and Frère Champney. New York [etc.]: G. P. Putnam's Sons, 1921. xiv, 352 p. front. plates. ports. 8°.

Scattered.

Love and death; three tragic scenes drawn from the works of Alexander Pushkin. In: Plays of the Moscow Art Theatre Musical Studio. New York, [cop. 1925.] vi, 27 p. 12°.

Contents: Aleko.—The fountain of Bakhchi-Sarai.—Cleopatra.

[Verses.] In: Deutsch, B., and A. Yarmolinsky. Russian poetry; an anthology. Chosen and translated by Babette Deutsch and Avrahm Yarmolinsky. New York: International Publishers, 1930. 254 p. new and rev. ed. 12°. p. 29-45.

Contents: A nereid.—"Behold a sower went forth to sow."—The

coach of life.—The prophet.—Message to Siberia.—Three springs.—Antiar.—Verses written during a sleepless night.—May 26, 1828.—Work.—Autumn.—A fragment.—Madonna.—Parting.

The captain's daughter and other tales, by Alexander Pushkin. London [etc.]: J. M. Dent & Sons, Ltd., [1933.] xi, 266 p. 16°. Everyman's library. Fiction. [no. 898.] Translated with introduction by Natalie Duddington. Bibliographical notes, p. x.

Contents: The captain's daughter.—The queen of spades.—Dubrovsky.—Peter the Great's negro.—The station master.

Poetry: Remembrance; I loved you. . . . [Translated by Maurice Baring.] The bronze horseman (A tale of Petersburg). [Translated by Oliver Elton.] Slavonic and East European Review, 1934. v. 13. p. 1-14.

Verse from Pushkin and others, by Oliver Elton. London: E. Arnold & Co., 1935. 188 p. 12°.

Pushkin, p. 27-170.

A collection of short lyrics, by Pushkin. Done into English verse by Mary Kremer Gray. From the literal translation of Ivan Panin. Hartford, Conn.: Privately printed, 1936. 24 p. front. (port.) 8°.

"Biographical" note, one page.
"Bibliography," at end.

The Russian wonderland: * Coq d'or; The tale of the fisherman and the fish; The tale of Czar Saltan. A metrical translation from the Russian of Alexander Poushkin, by Boris Brasol. . . . With an introduction by Clarence A. Manning. Published for the Poushkin Fund, Inc., New York: The Paisley Press, Inc., 1936. ix, 62 p. 80°

The works of Alexander Pushkin: lyrics, narrative poems, folk tales, plays, prose. Selected and edited, with an introduction, by Avrahm Yarmolinsky. New York: Random House, cop. 1936. viii, 896 p. 12°.

II. Individual Works Arranged Alphabetically in Chronological Order

The avaricious knight. Translated by Ernst J. Simmons.

(Harvard studies and notes in philology and literature, 1933. v. 15. p. 329-344.)

The Bakschesarian fountain. By Al. Pooschkeen. Translated from the original Russian by Will. D. Lewis. Philadelphia: C. Sherman, 1849. 72 p. 12°.

Boris Godunov. A drama in verse, by Alexander Sergyeyevicn Pushkin. Rendered into English verse by Alfred Hayes, with preface by C. Nabokoff. . . . London [etc.]: K. Paul, Trench, Trubner & Co., Ltd., [1918.] vi, 117 p. 12°.

Boris Godunov. London: British Russian Gazette, Trade Outlook, Ltd., 1935. 167 p. 8°.

The captain's daughter; or, The generosity of the Russian usurper, Pugatscheff. From the Russian of Alexander Puschkin, by G. G. Hebbe. . . . New York: C. Müller, 1846. 48 p. 8°.

The captain's daughter. . . . Translated by J. F. Hanstein. London, 1859. 8°.

Marie: a story of Russian love. From the Russian of Alexander Pushkin, by Marie H. de Zielinska. Chicago: Jansen, McClurg & Co., 1877. 209 p. 16°.

Published in 1846 under the title: The captain's daughter.

The captain's daughter. From the Russian of Pushkin. New York: G. Munro, [1883.] 101 p. 12°. Seaside library. Pocket ed. no. 149.

Published in 1877 under title: Marie.

The captain's daughter; a tale of the time of Catherine II of Russia. From the Russian of Poushkin translated by Madame Igelström and Mrs. Perey Easton. London, 1883. 244 p. 8°.

The daughter of the commandant; a Russian romance. Translated by Mrs. Milne Home. London: Eden & Co., 1891. 280 p. 8°.

The captain's daughter, by Alexander Pushkin. Translated from the Russian by Natalie Duddington, with an introduction by Edward Garnett. London: J. M. Dent & Sons, 1928. x, 212 p. 12°.

The captain's daughter, by Alexander Pushkin. Translated from the Russian by Natalie Duddington, with an introduction by Edward Garnett. New York: The Viking Press, Inc., 1928. x, 212 p. 12°.

Le coq d'or. Translated into English and copyrighted by Boris Brasol. (The first time ever printed.) [New York: Privately printed, 1932.] 4 l. 8°.

Don Juan. By Alexander Pushkin. Translated by Alexander Wert. (Slavonic Review, 1927. v. 5. p. 662-677.)

Dubrovsky, by Pushkin. In: Tales from the Russian. London, [1892.] 8°.

Eugene Oneguine; a romance of Russian life in verse, by Alexander Pushkin. Translated from the Russian by Lieut.-Col. Spalding. London: Macmillan and Co., 1881. xxiv, 276 p. 12°.

Biographical notice of Alexander Pushkin, p. xiii-xxiv.

Evgeny Onegin. Extracts translated from the Russian of Alexander Pushkin by Oliver Elton. (Slavonic Review. London, 1935. v. 13. p. 233-250.)

BIBLIOGRAPHY

Evgeny Onegin. Translated from the Russian by Oliver Elton. (The Slavonic Review, 1936. v. 14. no. 41. p. 249-269, continued in subsequent numbers.)

Mozart and Salieri. A dramatic poem by Alexander Pushkin. Translated from the Russian by Nicholas Lubimov. (Poet lore. Boston, 1920. v. 31. p. 297-304.)

Mozart and Salieri. (University of Toronto Quarterly, 1933. no. 4, p. 482-491.) Translated by A. F. B. Clark.

The pistol shot. In: Graham, S., ed. Great Russian short stories. New York: H. Liveright, 1929. xi, 1021 p. 8°. p. 29-42.

The post-master. In: Graham, S., ed. Great Russian short stories. New York: H. Liveright, 1929. xi, 1021 p. 8°. p. 43-45.

Queen of spades. Edited by D. Bondar. Oxford, 1917. (Oxford Russian plain texts.)

Queen of spades. Introduction by D. S. Mirsky, and original woodcuts in col. by H. Alexieff. . . . London: Backamore Press, 1929. 110 p. 4°.

The water nymph (Russalka). [Mount Vernon, N. Y., 191-?] 28 f. 4°. Translated by H. Badanes.

Caption title.

IV. OPERAS

Chaikovski, Piotr Il'ich, 1840-1893. Eugenio Oneghin; lyric opera in three acts, adapted from the poem of Pushkin. Music by P. Tschaikowski. New York: F. Rullman, Inc., [cop. 1920.] 37 p. 4°.

Libretto. Italian and English.

Musorgski, Modest Petrovich, 1835-1881. Boris Godounov; a musical drama in three acts. Music by M. Moussorgsky. New York: F. Rullman, Inc., [cop. 1911.] 51 p. 4°.

Libretto. Italian and English. Text as well as music by Musorgski. Based on drama by Pushkin with same title.

Musorgski, Modest Petrovich, 1839-1881. Boris Godunof; an opera in four acts with a prologue. The libretto translated into English by M. D. Calvocoressi. London: Oxford Univ. Press, 1929. vii, 58 p. 16°.

Libretto. English words. This edition gives in full both the initial version of Boris Godunof (1868-9) and the final version (1872).

Musorgski, Modest Petrovich, 1839-1881. Boris Godunof; an opera in four acts with prologue; the subject taken from A. S. Pushkin's dramatic chronicle bearing the same title, the greater part of the text of which is preserved. The complete original text edited in accordance with the autograph manuscripts, including hitherto unpublished scenes, episodes, fragments and variants, by Paul Lamm. English [and French] translation by M. D. Calvocoressi. Vocal score. Moscow: Music Section of the Russian State Pub. Dept., [cop. 1928.] xxiii, 458 p. tables. f°.

English and French words. Added t.-p. in French; editor's preface in English and French.

First performed in 1874. Libretto by Musorgski based on drama by Pushkin, and Karamzin's history of Russia.

VI. Works About A. S. Pushkin Arranged Alphabetically

Baring, Hon. Maurice, 1874-. Lost lectures; or, The fruits of experience, by Maurice Baring. London: P. Davies, 1932. 317 p. 8°.

Pushkin, p. 178-199.

Baring, Hon. Maurice, 1874-. An outline of Russian literature, by the Hon. Maurice Baring. London: Williams and Norgate, [1915.] vii, 256 p. 16°. (Home university library of modern knowledge. no. 99.)

Pushkin, p. 30-100.

Brasol, Boris Leo, 1885-. The mighty three: Poushkin, Gogol, Dostoievski. A critical trilogy by Boris Brasol. Introduction by Professor Clarence A. Manning. New York: W. F. Payson, 1934. xviii, 295 p. 8°.

Pushkin, p. 1-116.

Brasol, Boris Leo, 1885-. Poushkin, the Shakespeare of Russia. Address delivered on April 9, 1931, before the members of the Brooklyn Institute of Arts and Sciences. New York: Privately printed, 1931. 8 l. 8°.

Brueckner, Alexander, 1856-. A literary history of Russia, by A. Brückner. Edited by Ellis H. Minns. Translated by H. Havelock. London [etc.]: T. Fisher Unwin, 1908. xvii, 558 p. front. 8°. (The library of literary history. no. 9)

Pushkin, p. 178-210.

Dostoyevski, Fiodor Mikhailovich, 1821-1881. Pages from the journal of an author, Fyodor Dostoyevski. Translated by S. Koteliansky and J. Middleton Murry. Boston: J. W. Luce & Co., 1916. xiv, 117 p. 12°.

Pushkin: 1. A word of explanation concerning the speech on Pushkin, published below. 2. A speech delivered on 8th June 1880, at the meeting of the Society of Lovers of Russian literature, p. 33-117.

Hayes, Alfred, 1857-. Pushkin's "Boris Godunov." (Anglo-Russian Literary Society, London. Proceedings. 1918. no. 82, pp. 29-42.)

BIBLIOGRAPHY 243

Herford, Charles Harold, 1853-. The post-war mind of Germany, and other European studies, by C. H. Herford. Oxford: Clarendon Press, 1927. 248 p. 8°.
A Russian Shakespearian, p. 168-204.
Bibliographical footnotes.

Herford, Charles Harold, 1853-. A Russian Shakesperean; a century study. (John Rylands Library, Manchester. Bull. 1925. v. 9, p. 453-480.)

Herford, Charles Harold, 1853-. A Russian Shakesperean; a century study, by C. H. Herford. Manchester. The University Press. London, New York [etc.]: Longmans, Green & Co., 1925. 30 p. 8°.
Repr.: The bulletin of the John Rylands Library. v. 9. no. 2.
First of the Skemp memorial lectures at the University of Bristol.

Kropotkin, Piotr Alekseyevich, prince, 1842-1921. Ideals and realities in Russian literature, [by] Prince Kropotkin. New York: A. A. Knopf, 1915. vii. 341 p. 8°.
"This book originated in a series of eight lectures . . . delivered in March, 1901, at Lowell Institute."
Formerly published under title: Russian literature.
Pushkin, p. 39-50.

Kropotkin, Piotr Alekseyevich, prince, 1842-1921. Russian literature. New York: McClure, Phillips and Co., 1905. vii, 341 p. 8°.
Pushkin, p. 39-50.
Afterwards published under the title: Ideals and realities in Russian literature.

Manning, Clarence Augustus, 1893-. Alexander Sergeyevich Pushkin. (South Atlantic Quarterly, 1926. v. 25. p. 76-88.)

Manning, Clarence Augustus, 1893-. Russian versions of Don Juan. (The Modern Language Association of America. Publications. 1923. p. 479-493.)

Minayev, D. Eugene Onaigin of our times. (The Athenaeum, 1868. July 18. p. 73.)

Newmarch, Rosa. Poetry and progress in Russia, by Rosa Newmarch. . . . London: J. Lane, 1907. xvi, 269 p. front. ports. 8°.
"The romantic poets: Pushkin," p. 30-76: "Examples of Pushkin," p. 112-127.
"Examples" contain: The black shawl.—The upas tree.—To A. P. Kern.—The talisman. Translated by W. R. Morfill.—The high road in winter.—The roussalka.—Eastern song.—Tatiana's letter, from "Eugene Oniegin." Translated by Rosa Newmarch.—The duel, from "Eugene Oniegin." Translated by H. C. F.

Shaw, Thomas B. Pushkin, the Russian poet. (Blackwood's Edinburgh magazine, 1845. v. 57, p. 657-678; v. 58, p. 28-43.)

Spalding. A short biographical notice of Alexander Pushkin. In: Pushkin, A. S. Eugene Onéguine; a romance of Russian life. In verse. Translated from the Russian by Lieut.-Col. Spalding. London: Macmillan and Co., 1881. xxiv, 276 p. 8°. p. xii-xxiv.

Svyatopolk-Mirski, Dmitriĭ Petrovich, knyaz', 1890-. Modern Russian literature, by Prince D. S. Mirsky. London: Oxford Univ. Press, 1925. 120 p. front. ports. 12°. (The world's manuals.)
Pushkin, p. 7-13.

Svyatopolk-Mirski, Dmitriĭ Petrovich, knyaz', 1890-. Pushkin, by Prince D. S. Mirsky. London: G. Routledge & Sons, Ltd., 1926. front. (port.) 12°. (The Republic of Letters.)
Bibliography, p. 227-243.

Turner, Charles Edward. Studies in Russian Litteratur, by Charles Edward Turner. London: S. Marston, Searl and Rivington, 1882. viii, 389 p. 8°.
Pushkin, p. 209-317.

Vogüé, Eugène Marie Melchior, vicomte de, 1848-1910. The Russian novel, by le vicomte E.-M. de Vogüé. Translated from the eleventh French edition by Colonel H. A. Sawyer. With six portraits. London: Chapman and Hall, Ltd., 1913. iv, 335 p. 8°.
"Romanticism—Pushkin and poetry," p. 55-86.

Vogüé, Eugène Marie Melchior, vicomte de, 1848-1910. The Russian novelists, by E. M. de Vogüé. Translated by Jane Loring Edmands. Boston: D. Lothrop Co., [cop. 1887.] 275 p. 12°.
"Romanticism.—Pushkin and poetry," p. 44-55. "A list of English translations from the Russian," p. 273-275.

Addenda to Bibliography

Evgeny Onegin. Translated from the Russian of Alexander Pushkin, by Oliver Elton. Canto 2-3. [London: Eyre and Spottiswoode, Ltd., 1937.] 34 p. 8°.
Repr.: Slavonic Review. London. 1937. v. 15. no. 44.

Pushkin poetry: Stanzas to Mme Kern. Two fragments of "The czar Saltan." The prophet. The night. Antiar. The coach of life. Work. 'Tis time, my friend, 'tis time. Stanzas. To Joukovsky. A nereid. In: Pushkinskiye dni v Shankhaye. Pushkin centenary. English section. [Shanghai, 1927.] 109 p. 8°. p. 89-92.

Pushkin, 1799-1837. (The Vassar Review. Poughkeepsie, N. Y. 1937. February. p. 1-44.)

BIBLIOGRAPHY 245

Contents: H. N. MacCracken, Foreword.—Pushkin, A. S., Egyptian nights.—The fisherman and the fish.—Scene from "Faust."—Beckwith, M. W. Pushkin's relation to folklore.—Turgenev, I., What Pushkin merits from Russia.—Monnier, M., The dawn of Russian literature in France.—Fahnstock, E., "The stone guest" of Pushkin.—Dostoyevski, F., Pushkin's genius for understanding.—Flanagan, H., Pushkin and a people's theater.—Mestechin, N., Pushkin's text in the works of some Russian composers.—Bèm, A., The universal significance of Pushkin.—Strelski, N., Biographical note on Pushkin.—Bibliography.—Outline of world events contemporary with Pushkin. Compiled by members of the faculty and students.

Pushkin poetry: Stanzas to Mme Kern. Two fragments of "The czar Saltan." The prophet. The night. Antiar. The coach of life. Work. 'Tis time, my friend, 'tis time! Stanzas. To Joukovsky. A nereid. In: Pushkinskiye dni v Shankhaye. Pushkin centenary. [Shanghai, 1937.] 109 p. 8°. p. 89-92.

Pushkin and his works. In: Pushkinskiye dni v Shankhaye. Pushkin centenary. English section. [Shanghai, 1937.] 109 p. 8°. p. 81-88.

Simmons, Ernest Joseph, 1903-.

Pushkin, by Ernest J. Simmons. Cambridge, Mass.: Harvard Univ. Press, 1937. 485 p. facsims., front., plates, ports. 8°.

DATE DUE

PG 3350 .A4 P83 1971

Pushkin

3214

artist

HOUGHTON COLLEGE LIBRARY - Houghton, NY
1000175585